WHO KILLED MOM?

A *Delinquent* SON'S
**Meditation on Family, Mortality,
and Very Tacky Candles**

Steve Burgess

Who Killed Mom?

GREYSTONE BOOKS

D&M PUBLISHERS INC.

Vancouver/Toronto/Berkeley

Greystone Books
An imprint of D&M Publishers Inc.
2323 Quebec Street, Suite 201
Vancouver BC Canada V5T 4S7
www.greystonebooks.com

Cataloguing data available from Library and Archives Canada
ISBN 978-1-55365-833-7 (pbk.)
ISBN 978-1-55365-834-4 (ebook)

Editing by Peter Norman
Copyediting by Lara Kordic
Cover and text design by Jessica Sullivan
Cover photograph courtesy of Steve Burgess
Printed and bound in Canada by Friesens
Text printed on acid-free, 100% post-consumer paper
Distributed in the U.S. by Publishers Group West

We gratefully acknowledge the financial support of the Canada Council
for the Arts, the British Columbia Arts Council, the Province of British
Columbia through the Book Publishing Tax Credit, and the Government
of Canada through the Canada Book Fund for our publishing activities.

Cover photo: Summer 1959, Collins, Ohio. Front row—
Leslie Burgess, Lynn Burgess, and the author, already displaying
the writer's pensive air. Behind—Joan Burgess, with Fritz the
miniature dachshund, who goes cruelly unmentioned in this book.
He was a fierce family protector, and loved many a leg.

To dedicate this book to my parents, Bill and Joan Burgess, would be presumptuous, since it is in fact one of their many gifts to me.

So I dedicate it to Shelley Youngblut, who told me it was a book.

CONTENTS

1 Expiry Dates *1*

2 The Gift That Keeps on Rebuking *10*

3 Casablanca Christmas *26*

4 Grandma *34*

5 The Food Chain *45*

6 Made on a Friday *57*

7 A Bumpy Ride *71*

8 Regina *83*

9 Christmas Town *99*

10 Spoon und Drang *112*

11 Who Killed Mom? *125*

12 Trials *141*

13 Who Killed Grandma? *158*

14 Luck *167*

15 A Night in the Life *179*

16 Riverheights Terrace *188*

17 Parables of Joan *199*

18 End Game *213*

19 Time Trials *224*

20 Goodbye, Christmas Town *238*

Acknowledgements *251*

1

EXPIRY DATES

A LAST CHECK before heading to the airport. There are several containers of
yogurt in the fridge. I am wondering if I should just leave
them in hopes they'll still be good when I get back. And
that's what the situation has come down to—trying to
calculate whether yogurt or my mother will expire first.

After a long decline, the end is coming in a rush. Only
a week ago the family had still been in fight mode. There
had been a conference call organized by Brandon General Hospital. All five kids chiming in from the length
and breadth of North America, and at the hospital, Dad,
the home care nurses, and the doctor, sitting around a
speaker phone, discussing strategies. Even Mom attended,
wheeled down the hall from her hospital bed. Out on the
splayed ends of those phone lines we argued and discussed and all the while, in the gaps, listened for Mom's
voice—some evidence of consciousness and participation.
"Mom says hi," Dad offered near the end of the session.

Well, maybe she had. If so, the sound had not survived the journey to the far reaches of the continent.

By now we are seasoned ward warriors. This latest crisis is just one of the many that have previously landed Mom in hospital with a veritable chef's salad of mysterious symptoms. Mom's last few years have been a slow, fearful creep down a rotten staircase—incremental declines and the occasional catastrophic plunge. Almost eighty-three years old, she is suffering from severe Parkinson's, esophageal and thyroid problems, a possible brain lesion, and restless leg syndrome. Mom's got everything short of Lou Gehrig's disease, which is a shame. She always loved baseball.

Boxing, however, was never Mom's sport. That's a shame too. She deserves to be a regular on ESPN. Mom has managed more comebacks than Evander Holyfield. This is a woman who was not supposed to survive her thirteenth year. Over the years clumsy surgeries collapsed her lung, broke her ribs, severed one of her vocal cords, and damaged her esophagus. And that was the era we now call the good old days.

Lately Parkinson's has calcified her limbs, turning her body rigid even as her mind has been plagued by operational failures and intermittent system dropouts. Her weight slipped below ninety pounds—the difficulty of simply swallowing had put her in danger of starvation. It became necessary to surgically install a peg in her abdomen. Twice a day she sits in an easy chair while a home care nurse connects her to a feeding tube, through which a bag of high-calorie meal-replacement fluid drains directly into her stomach. She is now taking in nutrients in a manner more common to single-celled life forms. On the plus side, she never gets tired of vanilla.

The feedings can take up to forty-five minutes—a long, leisurely lunch as envisioned by some hack sci-fi screenwriter. Reading is not an option, since she can no longer focus on a printed page. A woman who was once a respected teacher, community leader, and the linchpin of her family has been reduced to the life of a pit pony, wearing a path from bed to feeding chair and back. It's helping—her weight has rebounded. But if she really was a boxer Mom would need two weeks of Twinkies and ice cream just to qualify for the junior flyweight division.

Still, she fights. Only months ago she had rallied herself to dress in her finest and sit down at a Christmas dinner table, her tiny spoonfuls of soup entering orally as nature intended, a triumphant communion accomplished through force of will. Three days later she managed it again, raising a shaky toast on the occasion of her fifty-eighth wedding anniversary. Best of all, New Year's Eve had seen her rise from her wheelchair to execute a careful, shuffling waltz with her old lover. "Her face just lit up when we danced," Dad says.

"I was dancing," Mom whispered to the home care nurse.

Now it is February and she is in hospital again. We know the drill—the name of the game is to agitate. The target: Mom's doctor. We five children neither like nor trust him. In recognition of his skill and relative stature in our eyes we have come to call him Dr. Molecule. Dad thinks we're too hard on Molecule, but the rest of us have more faith in Lynn—my eldest sister is a television producer and tireless researcher. When Parkinson's symptoms first began appearing in Mom, it was Lynn who came up with the diagnosis. Dr. Molecule dismissed her opinion. "Your mother is just getting old," he said.

Time passed; the situation deteriorated. Finally there came an appointment where Molecule sat in his office with Mom and Lynn, discussing my mother's latest symptoms. "Well, it's all part of Parkinson's disease," he said, almost in passing.

"So," Mom said, looking sideways at Lynn, "I have Parkinson's?"

"Yes, yes," Molecule replied.

Mom took some grim satisfaction from it. "At least he said it."

Perhaps we should be counting our blessings. If Doc Molecule had jumped on board the Parkinson's diagnosis right away, he might have prescribed Mirapex. An anti-Parkinson's drug approved in 1997, Mirapex has inspired a flurry of lawsuits. Alleged side effects include unbridled sexual urges and compulsive gambling. We didn't need that. Besides, Mom simply didn't have the necessary range and mobility to make the most of it.

Our generally hostile stance toward Molecule lent an adversarial air to medical consults. Doctor M. doesn't like Burgesses anymore than they like him. So the teleconference has a testy air. We lobby for health care services, try to undercut any hint of defeatism, and make plans for Mom's return home just as soon as she can get out of bed.

But that will never happen. Just days after the phone conference Lynn receives another call. It's a nurse on Mom's ward, calling secretly. We are not getting the true picture, the nurse says. Mom is now in a steep decline— in a coma, essentially. We need to make plans. When it comes from the nurse we believe it.

Now my two brothers are desperately rearranging schedules. By the time my sister Leslie and I arrive in Brandon, Lynn has been there for days, sitting up nights in Mom's room, alert to any change in her frightening, gasping breath. Mom looks wasted and frail. But it's that breathing that is the real shock—sharp, convulsive intakes of air, accentuated by the plastic echo chamber covering her mouth. You hear it, see her muscles convulse with the effort, and think: "It can't go on for long."

To add another pathology to the pile, Mom has developed double pneumonia. It's the pale horse that walks through these wards, carrying away the weak and compromised. Our established mistrust of medical opinion has been dissolved by the inevitable, by the heaving chest muscles that push out each breath.

My mother's death will not be a tragedy. As a family we are not dealing with the premature loss of a young life. There will be no agonizing decisions about organ donation, unless there's a ninety-four-year-old somewhere out there in need of a kidney.

Friends of mine have suffered real tragedies. Laura lost her mother to a drunk driver. Matthew's mother got early-onset Alzheimer's while still in her forties, leaving him with a stock of horrible yet sometimes blackly funny tales from his mother's rapid descent.

One story: The family is watching *Pretty Woman* on video when Matthew's mother becomes upset. Onscreen, Richard Gere has just asked Julia Roberts to go home with him. "I won't!" Matthew's mother shouts at the screen. The tape is rewound so that everyone can hear Roberts's response, and so Gere asks his question again. Matthew's mother is incensed. "You asshole!" she shouts. "I just told you no!"

We have been luckier, but luck runs out eventually. We drift in and out of Mom's hospital room, saying our futile hellos and watching her heavy, muscular respiration.

The progress of Parkinson's did not destroy Mom's personality. But, like a broken hard drive, the contents of her mind became hard to access. As things got worse Mom couldn't find words she needed. Speaking became a painful chore, concentration possible only in brief bursts followed by long sleeps. Mom was still there, somewhere, but that realization seemed more and more hypothetical as her interface software gradually failed. Attempts to communicate with her eventually came to seem selfish, meeting our own emotional needs at the expense of a tired, struggling woman who was using all her remaining resources just to keep functioning.

Now function simply means breath and circulation. And yet it has only been a week since her voice was heard. It happened one night when Dad was preparing to leave the hospital for the evening. "Here's a goodnight kiss," he told her, and then delivered three.

"You said just one," Mom whispered.

Wisecracking to the end. And those were in fact the last words anyone had heard from her.

I volunteer to take the overnight vigils. Nights are quiet in the palliative care ward. I sit beside Mom's bed, holding her hand as we watch TV. It feels oddly comfortable, like old times.

The woman on the bed is my mother. I know that. But she is an obstacle too, someone who has come between my mother and me. I have to look past her to see the woman who raised me, the woman I joked with so easily, the woman whom I admired above all others. Living in the moment is a necessity when you are dealing with medical crises, and as the family has responded to the series of setbacks that have taken our mother down the staircase to this moment we have slowly, almost unconsciously, adjusted to what she has become. There have been little deaths along the way—the realization that Mom will never again be able to come out and visit, the realization that she can no longer be counted on as the infallible personal assistant always capable of remembering the daily details we might have forgotten, the slow relinquishment of her position as the most trusted organizer and overseer of our lives. Then harder losses, among them the realization that Mom can no longer summon the attention and energy necessary to simply appreciate her children's and grandchildren's activities. As her Parkinson's gained ground, Mom was left running on emergency backup power.

And yet when she could manage a whispered quip in her desiccated voice we knew she was still there. Even more telling was her relationship with people who had known her only near the end—home care nurses, staff at the seniors' apartment complex my parents had moved into a couple of years before. They loved her, it was clear. To me it had seemed the cruellest blow that this woman who had taught English to countless students, who had cherished nothing more than gathering with intimate friends for conversation, who valued sincere and searching discussion, who took joy in any expression of common humanity and spirit, had seen her ability to communicate wither away.

But she was still communicating, somehow. I'd seen it during an earlier hospital stay, at a time when Mom was fighting illness and her decreasing mobility. A new nurse had come in after a shift change and begun bustling around the room. I barely noticed. But Mom engaged with her immediately. "I'm Joan," she said weakly. "What is your name?"

Dignity does not require language. People understand who she is. I try to take comfort from that. But it's hard. The new realities are driving out the old memories, of which I am jealously protective.

ALL OF JOAN BURGESS'S children have their memories. Some are commonly held, stories collectively shaped, tossed about, and rounded off over years of retelling. This one is mine: I am sitting on the floor, watching the last of the other kids go off to school. I don't start kindergarten until next year. And I am thinking, "This afternoon, Mom and I will go shopping." When five siblings are packed into a tight chronological group, undivided parental attention is gold.

Some people are heterosexual; some are homosexual. Lately my love life has been hypothetical. My brothers and sisters all settled down and started families. I never did. There have been some promising girlfriends along the way, but somehow I never managed to achieve domestic stasis. Pop psychologists love to pick over cases like mine. What combination of malign traits, internal defects, or perhaps personal hygiene issues keeps an apparently healthy man single?

I've heard enough theories to baffle the Warren Commission. This one might be as good as any: Perhaps somewhere deep in my subconscious, I was determined to replicate that brief, wonderful year when my siblings were all in school and I was the only kid at home. All my romantic ineptitude, all my ineffectual, fumbled attempts to find true love are thus explained—I was sabotaging myself. That way, I could keep going home to spend Christmas with my parents.

While my brothers and sisters have spent holidays in their own homes with their own children, every year I have returned to Brandon. Christmas is for kids, and there's a loophole hidden in there—no expiry date. A fifty-year-old trick-or-treater would not go over well, but Christmas is different. You can always go home.

Mom, Dad, and I, spending relaxed holidays at home, year after year. Decembers passed by in the family bungalow at 54 Clement Drive, pleasantly indistinguishable, the three of us well settled in a beloved routine. Decorations, some dating to the Eisenhower administration; driving excursions around the snow-packed streets to check out the light displays; punch and snacks and presents on Christmas Eve. Maybe *The Sound Of Music* will be on TV again—maybe it's a dead certain lock. Maybe for certain I will groan and smirk and make sure to sit where no one will detect signs of localized precipitation when Captain von Trapp sings "Edelweiss." Better yet, perhaps we'll watch Alastair Sim in *Scrooge*, the only film version of Dickens's *A Christmas Carol* that should be legally authorized for broadcast.

All sweetly predictable—until three years ago. On that particular December 24 we would be visited by Dickens's most terrifying spirit. The Ghost of Christmas Yet to Come has a thankless gig—he knows that good news is always temporary. Stare far enough into the future, and the outlook is always grim.

2

THE GIFT THAT
KEEPS ON REBUKING

I NEVER DECORATE my Vancouver apartment in December. Why bother? Christ-
mas doesn't live there. It lives with my parents in the
town where I grew up. Brandon is Christmas Town. We
are fundamentalists. Not Christian fundamentalists—
Christmas fundamentalists. On key doctrinal issues
such as who sits where, what snacks will be available, and
which thirty-year-old cheesy decoration goes on which
table, unyielding fanaticism is the rule. The Santa candles
were a case in point.

Every year the standard elements are put in place.
There is the party mix—Cheerios, Shreddies, pretzels,
peanuts, all baked with butter—and Mom's fruit punch.
Come the New Year, there's always enough leftover punch
to fill a bathtub. Once we got older it became more important as a concept than as an actual beverage.

Any proposed changes to the routine must be sub-
mitted to a standard arbitration process, beginning with

howls of outrage, proceeding through accusations of heresy, complete rejection, and finally an apology for having brought them up. Once a little electric candelabra got tossed out, but that followed several arcing episodes and, I believe, a call from the fire marshal.

But the Santa candles? There was nothing wrong with those. Four little Santas posing around the letters N-O-E-L. We never lit them, and it's not like wax goes bad. So what would possess anyone to throw them out? What? It was a senseless crime. You hear about such outrages on the news, but you never think one will be committed by your own mother.

Apparently Mom had it in for those poor Santas all along. She must have. One year they were just gone. Fundamentalist outrage ensued. Unfortunately for Mom, it happened that Lynn had also come home for Christmas that year. Together we plotted revenge. Fanning out through the Brandon Shoppers Mall, we purchased every Santa candle we could lay hands on—short, tall, old school, hot pink. Each vengeful Claus was wrapped and placed under the tree. Mom was opening them up all night, one after another. "Another Santa candle!" she would say brightly, fixing Lynn and me with a rictal grin. They were the gifts that kept on rebuking.

She kept them all. Some of the old-fashioned ones are actually rather attractive. In time they too became part of the fundamentalist tradition.

Not much happens in our Christmas routine, but it's all crucial. Christmas Eve we go to church. Not standard procedure for me, but it's a social event. Once home, Dad sits in his rocking chair pulled up beside the tree. Mom is to his left while I sit on the floor to the right. One by one the gifts are picked up, and the tags read out in Dad's sonorous baritone. Each gift must be sufficiently fussed over before the next can be picked up. Phone calls from Burgess outposts periodically interrupt the action. It all takes hours.

Through changing circumstances and practical difficulties we have struggled to maintain our cherished routine. It hasn't always been simple. The struggles started early. I was only a couple of years away from home, working as a radio announcer in Estevan, Saskatchewan, the low man on the staff list. Even at an Estevan radio station, one can lack status relative to others. Remember Jonathan Swift:

> So, naturalists observe, a flea
> Has smaller fleas that on him prey;
> And these have smaller still to bite 'em;
> And so proceed ad infinitum.

In Estevan I was about five fleas down the depth chart. That meant working over Christmas. The shift schedule had me on air December 24 until noon, and then again at noon on Christmas Day. When I got off shift on the twenty-fourth, Dad was waiting outside the station with the engine running. We drove the three hours to Brandon, had a lovely Christmas Eve, and drove back next morning.

Years later the same situation at an Edmonton radio station required more drastic measures, 632 miles being too long a drive. So Christmas itself was delayed until I could get home. A mammoth task, made easier today by time-shifting technology that allows *The Sound of Music* and *A Charlie Brown Christmas* broadcasts to be recorded and stored. Back in the day, delaying Christmas was more about denial and drawing the drapes.

There was another year in which Christmas Eve had to be delayed. It wasn't a matter of circumstances—it was a matter of I screwed up, big.

I had moved to Vancouver to DJ at another radio station, and managed to get a few days off over Christmas. I booked a flight home for the twenty-fourth. A cheap charter flight, since I am by nature a cheapskate. But even these savings were not enough. I decided to save even more. Instead of forking out for a cab to the airport I hopped a city bus, leaving myself about ninety minutes' lead time. It's hard to feel sympathy for anyone that stupid, but I ask you to try. The bus was packed. Every single block the cord would be pulled, the bell would ring, and the bus would trundle over to the curb like some drooling Pavlovian beast. The clock jogged on. My brain was screaming. A city bus to the airport? It was like trying to make a quick sandwich with flour, yeast, and a package of tomato seeds. Finally I jumped off, waving frantically at passing cabs. It was too late. By the time I arrived it was less than half an hour before departure—the gates had closed on my charter flight. Despite my carefully calibrated attempt to pry them open by screaming abuse at an attendant, they stayed closed.

When I called home to explain, I was surprised to find myself choking up. It was a lesson, and not just about public transit. Vancouver Airport was eerily quiet on Christmas Day, populated by shift workers and perhaps a few screw-ups like me. Getting a standby seat was no problem. I made it to Brandon a day late. Christmas Eve was pushed back to Christmas night and may even have gained some richer flavour from the extra day's ripening. Certainly my unexpected swell of emotion on the phone had been for me a gift. It was a re-dedication of sorts, a new commitment to our Christmas ritual.

Later that charter airline went out of business. So it all worked out.

Once I learned to spring for cabs, our Christmases rolled on for years with few hitches. Yet in hindsight it seems that we may as well have lit those old Santa candles. You hang on to the totems and traditions, but ultimately it's like trying to hold on to your drink in a plane crash. Everything must go.

Dad's health suffered first. In 1999 a heart attack led to a sextuple bypass operation—more bypasses than there are arteries. It must look like a map of Dallas–Fort Worth in there.

It was our introduction to a new reality, a new era of sudden phone calls that reel us back from separate worlds to gather and wait and fret. One of my strongest memories from that first crisis was the sight of all of us in Dad's hospital room, and Mom propped up beside him on the bed. For a woman as reserved as our mother, it was the equivalent of making out on a park bench.

Dad's rewired fuse box held up well enough, but at his age trouble always has plenty of options. A few years later came the next mess—an abdominal aneurysm. Recovery from surgery was hard. His short-term memory was going and, thanks to macular degeneration, so was his eyesight. In the face of that onslaught, even the strongest traditions must give way. It was at Dad's earnest request that I reluctantly took over his Christmas Eve spot in the rocking chair, handing out the gifts. I was Santa now. It didn't feel right—I sat in that Christmas throne as uneasily as Macbeth.

Meanwhile his memory issues became a topic of debate. According to Doc Molecule, Dad was suffering from early stage Alzheimer's. He rejected the diagnosis with a rare vehemence. "I don't have that," he insisted, unwilling even to say the word. But we braced ourselves. Whether it was truly the "A" word or just memory loss brought on by poor circulation—vascular dementia— Dad's short-term memory was now a very leaky bucket.

To sit watching *Eternal Sunshine of the Spotless Mind* with my Dad became a true meta-movie experience. The film, directed by Michel Gondry from a script by Charlie Kaufman, involves a fictional company that can erase specific memories from the brain, wiping out all traces of a bad relationship or traumatic event. Kaufman is renowned for scripts, like *Adaptation* and *Being John Malkovich*, that blur the line between fiction and reality. He would have been thrilled to watch *Eternal Sunshine* with my father. It was better than 3-D, a virtual mind warp in which the disappearing memories on screen mixed and collided with the forgetfulness of the viewer in a storm of synaptic misadventure. "Who's that again?" Dad asked. "Is this the same guy we saw before? Who's this woman? Is she real? Is this part real?"

Kaufman would have been inspired. With the right sort of audience he could have transformed a mere movie into an interactive event. Watching a hockey game with Dad, though, was just annoying. "Okay, are we the team in red? Right. Now—which team are we? The guys in white? No. Got it . . . which ones are we cheering for, again?"

With our focus on Dad, Mom's decline went unnoticed at first. Perhaps it was not something we even wanted to acknowledge. Once, during a visit to Vancouver, she had confided in me. "I know I'm slipping," she said. "My mental processes are not the same."

I reassured her, dismissing her concerns. She was telling me something, and I wasn't listening. It would be evident soon enough. My parents had enjoyed a long and healthy retirement. But that seemed to be over now. Medically, they were suddenly in a race to the bottom.

Unexpectedly, Mom grabbed the lead. A series of accelerating crises began. Mom had always contended with medical issues. She had experienced thyroid problems and a lifelong difficulty with swallowing. An operation intended to correct her esophageal trouble had not only failed but made matters considerably worse by disabling the muscles that allowed for peristalsis, the action of pushing food downward. Henceforth she would have to get by on gravity and fluids. For good measure, the surgeon accidentally broke her rib and collapsed her lung. A later operation on her thyroid had led to a surgeon slicing one of her vocal chords, permanently affecting her voice. If we had been Americans we could have lived like kings off malpractice money. (Not that Mom would ever have sued. She once refused to accept a prize of Saskatchewan Roughriders season tickets because she thought it was wrong to gamble. Or something like that—the rest of us were too appalled to hear clearly.)

As for Dr. Molecule, he had a standard take on things: "Your mother is just getting old."

Our disillusionment grew. And yet our attempts to get a new doctor were unsuccessful, always running up against professional courtesy. "She's Dr. Molecule's patient," other doctors would tell us. "I couldn't take her."

Dr. Gunsen was a psychiatrist who attended Knox Church. After watching Mom walk out of church one Sunday, he had a quiet word with Lynn. She typed that word into a search engine and found herself looking at a familiar list of symptoms. It was Parkinson's.

Meanwhile, medical perils accumulated. There was a rash of sudden falls, one of which left Mom with a broken wrist. Another Sunday she went down hard in the Knox lobby, her head smacking the hard floor with a resounding crack. Dr. Gunsen was the first to reach her. "I'm a head doctor," he explained. Mom laughed, which was good.

At one point she developed near-total insomnia. The intrepid Lynn diagnosed an overdose of thyroid medication, but the problem would not be addressed until an emergency trip to the ER, where her thyroid medication was adjusted by the on-call doctor. Those ER trips were the only way Mom could get a second opinion—that, and falling down in church.

Matching Mom's symptoms with conditions was like tracing the paternity of a stray cat. Eventually a brain scan revealed some sort of unidentified growth in her head. Then there was restless leg syndrome—weird, electric jitters running through her legs, a nightly torment that drove her to walk the floors at all hours.

I habitually kept late hours, and so during my Christmas trips home I would be up watching TV when she came shuffling into the kitchen, trying to walk off the jitters. Thus was born the Peach Marathon.

Mom liked canned peaches. They were easy to swallow. Sometimes she'd have a couple of them before returning to bed. One night as she paced around the kitchen I opened up a new can of peaches for her. She described slow circles around the dishwasher, and after each lap I offered up peach morsels on a fork. She would pause to accept a bit of peach, and do another circuit. One lap, one piece of peach. "A trained seal," she mused. "It's not a bad life."

Pretty soon it became a new routine. When I heard her footsteps in the night I would head for the can opener like a cat.

You can never imagine what circumstances will present. Nor can you imagine that you will shortly look back on such odd, diminished situations with fondness. But the new normal is always resetting the bar lower. Somewhere along the way the annual Christmas celebrations changed character. Once a tally of passing years, they had become a countdown.

Christmas 2006 would be a master class in the new realities. Dad had spent some of November and most of December in hospital, his heart waffling and quibbling and generally refusing to settle into a steady narrative. With the exact problem eluding proper diagnosis we were just waiting for the situation to clear up on its own. As I headed for the airport he was still in captivity, still the subject of inconclusive tests.

We got him home with just days to spare. As a holiday spice, long hospital stays will probably never be popular. But they lend an undeniable kick. There was some extra savour to all our cherished rituals.

The night before Christmas Eve, there was a knock on the door. Jostling on the front steps was a gang of carollers. Dad had missed a few practices adding his bass notes to the choir at Knox United, so they decided to make a house call.

Dad tended to inspire that kind of love and loyalty. One year he had suffered from a case of shingles so painful he couldn't wear a shirt. Friends invited him to a party—a nice gesture, yet for Dad a painful exercise in dressing up. Mom and Dad arrived early at the party and waited for their friends to arrive. Which they finally did, all at once, and all topless. "The women were just wearing bras," Dad recalls. "I guess the guys were topless too. I mostly remember the women."

The Knox choir serenaded us for a while. Then at Mom's instruction I fished out a bottle of rum and started mixing up eggnogs. People were asking for my secret. The secret: rum. Even Mom had a second one, which was very rare indeed. She was stepping out. For my part, the transgressive pleasure of the moment was simply to be on the supply side, serving up slightly-stronger-than-regulation drinks to my own mother. I had never seen her more than slightly flushed and bright-eyed from the effects of alcohol. And yet there was a history of alcohol abuse in our relationship—all of it originating from me. Those days were long gone and unlamented now. But even these many years later, there must have been a little extra holiday cheer for her just in knowing that the bartender was not sneaking rum shots on the side. All was well.

Still, the coming seasonal festivities called for some cautious monitoring. Dad was fresh out of hospital, and it had become clear that my mother was too frail and unsteady to do any two things consecutively. Two scheduled events always required an intervening nap. But Christmas Eve was coming, and tradition was unyielding. An exception could be made, surely.

ON THE NIGHT of the twenty-fourth we returned from church and moved directly into part two of the usual thing, nibbling snacks, drinking the fruit punch, opening presents till at least midnight. In the pleasant paper-strewn aftermath my mother shuffled off to the kitchen while Dad and I chatted. I cast a nervous glance after her—a recently developed habit. Behind Dad's voice I heard a crash and a lingering rattle. Twenty seconds of criminal indecision followed. Dad talked on, oblivious, while I wondered if I was worrying too much. Finally I headed for the kitchen.

Mom was crumpled on the floor, her head against the coffee cart that had rattled and banged like reindeer bells to announce this Christmas Eve landing. Her fancy red-and-black Christmas outfit was covered in eggnog. Her eyes blinked at the ceiling. I sat her down and sponged off her best black skirt. Ninety pounds at most, shaking uncontrollably, she was like a fallen baby bird.

I led her down the hall to her bedroom, slipping her out of her Christmas Eve clothes and tucking her into bed. Only then did I go back to the living room. "Mom's had a fall," I told Dad. He started out of his chair with a look that seemed equal parts guilt and fear. He felt it was his responsibility to notice things like this.

Back in the kitchen my tears came suddenly, like a bout of the shakes after a near-miss on the highway. This was no Christmas Eve of quiet joy. It was instead a visit from Dickens's terrible Spirit of Prophecy, pointing a bony finger toward the grave.

Months later when I mentioned the incident, Dad could not recall it. Whether it was a defence mechanism or just the new normal, it was disturbing.

I might have guessed that it would be our last Christmas at 54 Clement. I didn't, though, mostly because I didn't want to think too much about it. Events proceeded, regardless. That summer our home was swept away in a tornado of parental resolve.

The move was largely Mom's doing. Her familiar surroundings were becoming a source of fear. As she grew increasingly unsure of her own physical stability, the house with its stairs and space became an enemy. And so the final stage of the family's thirty-seven-year tenure in the house at 54 Clement Drive started with a recurring series of panic attacks and culminated in a two-week frenzy, a frantic centrifugal spin-off of furniture and knick-knackery in service of an abrupt parental decision.

Mom was now prone to hyper-anxiety. It could be triggered by incidents as minor as seeing Lynn reorganize her closet. Her decreasing ability to communicate made the reasons for her anxiety attacks hard to divine. We had to become alert to the signs—her breathing, her eyes. Mom was now hostage to her emotions. Was her anxiety the natural reaction of a woman who had always survived on tight self-discipline and personal control now finding herself stuck in the passenger seat of her own life? Was it the Parkinson's? Or was some other opportunistic disorder piling on to a weakened warrior?

One thing became clear—symptom or not, Mom was feeling panicky about the house. She wanted to look at seniors' facilities. The prospect of having to go down-stairs to the laundry room, risking serious falls, was a big issue. We discussed a plan to move everything onto one floor, which quieted the moving talk for a time. But the subject kept cycling back around—it seemed to be about more than just the laundry. Some little engine was driving Mom's anxiety around and around. Whether logic or disease, the little motor would give her no rest.

In the summer of 2007 Lynn and my brother Jock were in Brandon for a visit, planning a trip up to Clear Lake. One day Dad suggested they go for a tour of a new assisted living facility on the edge of town, a place called Riverheights Terrace. It proved to be an eventful day. On the way through the front door Mom tripped and fell hard. She completed the tour in a wheelchair. Before Lynn and Jock had fully grasped what was happening, Mom and Dad were in the manager's office signing a rental agreement. A relaxing visit to the lake was out. The rest of the trip would be spent planning a move.

They made some headway toward tidying and orga-nizing, preparing to put the house on the market, then flew home. Two days after Lynn got back to Toronto, Dad called. He had just signed a deal with a realtor. The house was to be vacated in two weeks.

With the other kids temporarily tied up, Lynn and Jock were now in the eye of the storm. Days after arriving home they were back out west and headfirst into a des-perate scramble—a fast-forwarded attempt to prioritize, pack, divide, divest, divvy up, donate, and dispose, paus-ing occasionally to mutter heartfelt prayers that someday a certain pushy realtor would fry in the everlasting fires of Hell.

Dad got less of the blame—he was easily influenced these days, stressed and feeling the push of Mom's anxi-ety. Nonetheless he was the one who had signed the agreement, and now he seemed oblivious to the panic around him. Dad acted on the moving process like a parachute on a drag racer. "You can't throw that out!" he would exclaim, regularly.

"Dad, it's a jar full of rusty hinges/bag full of plastic bags/box full of used batteries."

"Right! I might need those!"

Never before had I heard any of my siblings seething over a phone line with such distinct, crackling heat. Dad's childlike qualities have always been part of his charm— simplicity, enthusiasm, and an almost disingenuous faith in people. But his miserable short-term memory now combined with a certain suggestibility, lack of focus, and inability to prioritize. Not the man you wanted in charge of a major reorganization project.

One day Dad was given a bucket with an order to clean out some work drawers and separate the wheat from the chaff. He dutifully managed to throw some odds and ends into the garbage bucket—random widgets, pieces of plastic, old file cards, and so on. Returning several hours later, he looked into the garbage bucket and proceeded to bag up the contents for the move. The bucket, he figured, must contain the good stuff.

While Lynn and Jock continued to clear out the house, Mom and Dad took possession of the new apartment at Riverheights Terrace. Mom would be there for exactly one night.

Throughout the desperate effort to clear out the old house Lynn and Jock had watched Mom with growing concern. Frequently sleepless, she was given to massive anxiety attacks over concerns so minor that no one else could understand them. Past experience strongly suggested that Dr. Molecule would be unhelpful and dismissive. Lynn decided to attempt an end run by taking Mom to a walk-in clinic. "The doctor at the clinic looked at Mom and was overwhelmed. She said, 'This is too much for me. I wouldn't know where to start. She can't be treated here.'"

The night Mom and Dad relocated, Jock and Lynn returned to sleep in the empty house. In the early morning there was a knock on the door. A paramedic stood outside, bathed in the red strobe of the ambulance that stood idling on the street. The paramedics had just come from Riverheights—Mom had had another serious fall. Dad convinced them to stop by at 54 Clement and pick up Lynn and Jock on the way to the hospital.

Mom was delirious. She recognized no one, speaking only to herself. In her hospital bed she mimed repetitive motions, apparently taking a series of invisible pills. One day Lynn noticed that her wedding ring was missing from the bedside table. It would turn up later, on a stomach x-ray. If the nurses recovered it, we never found out.

Just what was going on was impossible to know. A neurologist did a CT scan and discovered some sort of mass in her brain—a tumour, he surmised. Then there was the Parkinson's (which Dr. Molecule had only recently, grudgingly, admitted as a proper diagnosis). But did Parkinson's cause this sort of prolonged delirium? Was it a drug reaction? Something connected to her ongoing thyroid issues? What about the panic attacks? We were at a loss, unable to trust our doctor and unable to escape from his clutches thanks to the professional courtesies of a tight-knit medical community.

The day before Jock and Lynn were scheduled to leave, there was a small miracle. Mom was sitting up in bed. She knew them, talked to them. Jock was almost overwhelmed. "That whole experience, all that trouble, was worth it for that day. We got Mom back."

I flew in for the next shift. I tended to be lucky that way—in most times of parental crisis Lynn was the first responder and ended up doing the grunt work, sleeping in chairs, fighting with obdurate medical personnel. Then I would arrive to spring the now-recovered parent from hospital and grab the glory.

So it would be this time. Landing at Winnipeg Airport in the early evening, I dropped a lead foot onto the gas pedal of my rental car, hoping to reach the hospital before the end of visiting hours. They let me go up anyway. I found Mom sleeping. She opened her eyes as I leaned over her, and started like the guest of honour at a surprise party. Then her brow furrowed. "Am I dreaming?" she asked earnestly.

It took a couple of weeks but we got her sprung. It was indeed a royal procession—into the wheelchair out to the car accompanied by song (I think I did an a cappella Herman's Hermits number), a stop at the Dairy Queen for the ritual ice cream cone so beloved by both my parents on summer evenings, then home to the new, westward-facing apartment in Riverheights, surrounded by balloons and flowers and excited, fussing friends. "I'll bet you didn't know you had so many people waiting for you," someone said.

"I do now," Mom said. "I feel very loved."

The house at 54 Clement Drive was a shell. Wandering through was not as hard as I'd expected. Naked rooms, pockmarked walls—it was a dead thing now. Getting rid of the contents was the hard part, and I had dodged that.

Still, it was chastening to have to take back Christmas gifts I had given my parents over the years—a perfume decanter from Morocco, a monk's begging bowl from Bangkok. They'd served their purpose, demonstrating that I thought of my folks while I was far away. Now they, along with countless other gifts and tokens of love, were detritus. The relentless generator that is Christmas, chugging away at the family home for thirty-seven years, had left emissions everywhere. Santa is never around when it's time to deal with his carbon footprint.

There's a lingering presence when you leave a home, like fingernails growing on a corpse. The solicitations keep arriving in the mailbox, the structural additions and backyard plantings remain, the uninformed still drop by. Now another Christmas is on the way and we are gone. Will it even find us? Will it be delivered to our old address and discarded with the ad mail?

No more Christmas fundamentalism for us. This Burgess Christmas will break new ground. It's unavoidable. Among other innovations, it will see me introduced to an old, and previously very casual, acquaintance.

3

:
:
:
:
:
:

CASABLANCA CHRISTMAS

CHRISTMAS IS here and there's no room at the inn. My parents' Riverheights Terrace home is a two-bedroom apartment. There are guest accommodations down the hall, but we were too slow to book, and I have to find temporary quarters for the holidays. Christmas iconography may suggest that I should bunk in a stable. I think I came pretty close. There's no manger here, but it's mangy.

My lodging is a motel located about half a mile down the road. When I was young it was called the Starlight. Under new management, it is now known as the Casablanca. The architecture betrays no Moroccan influences; there's no restaurant or room service, which rules out tangy lamb *tagine* with couscous. If Humphrey Bogart ever passed through Brandon he kept it quiet. The motel's not even white. Why is it called the Casablanca? Why is North Korea called the Democratic People's Republic? Why is New Jersey the Garden State?

In 1965, when the Burgess family arrived in Brandon, the Starlight Motel was already a relic, a victim of urban development. Its location on Victoria Avenue made perfect sense back when Victoria doubled as part of the Trans-Canada Highway, and the Starlight was the first option for weary Studebaker pilots headed east. Then the highway moved north, bypassing the expanding town that quickly swallowed up and digested the Starlight. Now, like a beached ship, the old motel sits in a primarily residential zone and has been re-christened the Casablanca. It's unlikely a bottle of champagne was wasted.

Even when I was a kid it seemed incongruous. Who would stay there? Trysting townies? Their cars would be easy enough to spot. For many years it was a couple of blocks away from the now-defunct Suburban Restaurant, the city's finest in an era when Baked Alaska was sophistication incarnate (and a name that invoked the suburbs apparently held some sort of cachet). As such it may have been a destination for tipsy celebrants playing it safe—except in those days nearly everybody on the road was half-drunk and thought little of it. So I don't know how it survived.

Maybe it was waiting for me. Maybe I used to be the caretaker. I always loved *The Shining*. As I drive up to the office it is clear I have one thing in common with Jack Nicholson at the Overlook Hotel—I am going to be the only resident. It's snowing too.

A short woman in cleaning togs hustles down the long sidewalk and enters the office. "Sorry," she says, "I just had to fire the cleaning woman. I'm Barb. My husband, Ralph, and I just took over managing the place. Just got here from Alberta."

As I fill out the form, she elaborates. "The previous manager was scamming the owner," she says. "Skimming off the top. Plus, he'd take a security deposit from a customer and then throw them out—tell them there was no drinking or something—and pocket the deposit. One old guy used to bring his Native gal here every week. He threw them out and kept their money. He's never come back."

Some places could fall back on the carriage trade. But the Casablanca needs its regulars. If the name change was intended to goose business, it wasn't working. No vehicles were parked along the long row of rooms.

Casablanca's Rick was plagued by Nazis; *The Shining's* Jack Torrance by madness. I am suffering a serious attack of lower-back pain. A firm mattress, I ask hopefully? "We're replacing them gradually," Barb says. "Last week there was a party, and I guess there was a fight. One fellow got hurt pretty bad, and the mattress was totally blood-soaked. So we had to replace that one."

I cross my fingers for that room.

I get 116, down at the end of the deserted row, a small, dowdy, but clean cubicle offering vintage carpet, wood panelling, fridge, microwave, TV, dead batteries in the largest remote I've ever seen, and a surprisingly good mattress. The calendar reads November. A framed quotation on the wall is taken from John 3:16 and not, as I expected, "All work and no play makes Jack a dull boy." The bathroom sink is an unpredictable beast, pooling up for long periods and then suddenly draining on a whim. But there are no visible vermin. Happily, it is much too cold outside for any crawly new arrivals. That offers one small advantage over my old bedroom in the family basement, which had been Palm Beach for wintering spiders.

On the way to my parents' new home, I drive past our former digs. The driveway at 54 Clement Drive is now home to two cars, a pick-up truck, and a basketball hoop.

Someone is busy making new traditions in the old place. Well, good for them. I have my very own chateau. I am an Eastern potentate, a journeying king of the Orient. I am Lord of the Casablanca.

None of the Burgess kids was prepared to embrace Riverheights. A new family address is like a new step-mom after a quickie divorce. This one came with a whole new family. Riverheights Terrace is an "assisted living" facility. Not a nursing home, but serviced apartments for seniors, with meals served in a communal dining room. What the food lacks in spice it makes up with an exciting hint of international air travel.

Food is not an issue for Mom these days—she's lucky in that at least. And yet, with the new state of affairs, even the cherished Christmas dinner is out, unless it can be pulverized and pumped through a tube.

We all recoiled at the feeding tube idea initially. Considered out of context it almost seemed too much. Circumstances alter cases, as legal beagles say. Mom had actually been drinking Ensure meal replacement for years on account of her lifelong swallowing problems. The complicating factor of Parkinson's had only made the situation more grave. Still, her low weight was somewhat deceptive—for Mom, weighing less than an NFL lineman's leg is not the issue it might be for someone else. The kind of weight problem Mom has battled all her life is not the one that has made Kirstie Alley famous. Eighty pounds is only twenty or thirty below Mom's normal. And now, thanks to the magic sci-fi feeding tube, she is back up to ninety. It has been a success. When the time comes you do what's needed. And you have the Christmas you can manage.

It's the old frog-in-a-boiling-pot story—increase the heat gradually and the frog never notices until he looks down and sees a French chef putting sauce on his legs. So it has been with Mom. Change has been incremental. And yet when you look back only a couple of short years, the transformation has been startling. Activities, abilities, key character traits have fallen away. Mom is still there, but her light shines fitfully, like a partly cloudy day.

Still, we're doing okay in our new Bethlehem. Some of the surprise element has leaked out of the whole Christmas Eve thing—Mom has asked me to take her down to Staples and point out a couple of items I might find useful, then briefly leave the store while she buys one. It's not a bad system. One day I express a liking for a fleece blanket in Dad's room, only to find it wrapped up and under the tree on Christmas Eve. Somehow that one gets me right in the tear ducts. Real "Gift of the Magi" stuff.

We celebrate the fifty-seventh anniversary with dinner out. Mom can at least order soup. All in all a lovely evening, if perhaps tiring for some. On the way home I am driving, with Mom in the passenger seat and Dad in the back. Conversation turns to the topic of a vintage coat—apparently it went missing in the move. "I think I gave it away," Mom says. "I gave it to..."

"Olivia?" Dad chimes in. Olivia is their grandchild, Lynn's teenage daughter.

"No," Mom says. "I know her..."

"Your home care nurse?" I suggest.

"No," Mom says, struggling. "Olivia's mother."

I freeze like a man who has just heard terrible news. The radio is playing and I hope Dad has been unable to hear our last exchange. "You mean Lynn?" I ask.

"Yes," she says.

We are silent for a moment. "I know the name," Mom says at last. "I can see the letters in my mind. But I just can't say them."

It's not Alzheimer's. Whatever is going on inside her brain seems more comparable to faulty wiring or broken connections. She has not forgotten the information, and yet somehow she cannot retrieve it.

"My world keeps getting smaller," she tells me one afternoon. It's undeniable. Her days are being gradually reduced to a country two-step: bed, feeding chair, back to bed. There's no return on this road, and she knows it. Even her ability to grasp those small pleasures left to her is deteriorating.

And yet not long ago she told Lynn, "There will never be enough time."

Hypothetical discussions are just that. Brave speculation about how you'll never put up with this or that indignity evaporates, and here you are in the present, hanging on. We want Mom to hang on. And she seems willing. My mother is a very tough bird. Nobody's quitting yet.

But then, no one in this world has it easy. Certainly not the new managers of the Casablanca. On my very first night I lose my key. It's after midnight, and I am forced to trudge down to the office and rouse Rick and Barb out of bed, stammering apologies. At least it isn't a knife fight.

All in all, the week has been okay. Christmas holiday at the Casablanca is still a hometown Christmas. A long shuffle down the Riverheights Terrace hallway is still a walk with my mother. The family home is gone—the family, as yet, is not. The old realities are sliding away, but that's a situation many grieving people wish they could have experienced. Some people's worlds end in a cataclysm, with sudden shocks and unbearable changes of circumstance. My family's world is adrift. A difficult transition to be sure, but perhaps a kinder one. There are worse things than Christmas Eve at the Casablanca, watching It's a Wonderful Life.

Although, the way our familiar old world is crumbling away, perhaps the flick should be *Gone With the Wind.*

MARCH 2009. I'm on night shift again in the palliative care ward, watching TV and holding Mom's hand, listening to her gulping breath.

Mom's last words have been spoken. We've had all we are going to get. And already I am surprised and frustrated by the difficulty I have in remembering things she said.

Mom was not the sort of joker who regaled a table with knee-slapping anecdotes. But not because she lacked a sense of humour. When comfortably among family and friends, Mom was more of a quiet quipper, taking pleasure in dryly witty banter. But not for her the big joke. Jokes are little performances, and Mom loathed being the centre of attention. Still, her counter-punching ability could always surprise, as it did one day while lunching with co-workers at the Assiniboine Community College. One of them was rambling on about animal husbandry. "If a castrated stallion is a gelding," he mused, "and a castrated ox is a steer, what would you call a castrated boar?"

"A bigger bore," Mom blurted out.

Mom and I loved to banter. Not the nasty one-upsmanship so beloved of frat boys, but just a gentle back-and-forth quipping. On those occasions when I might have been teasing her about something, she would always go along with the theme rather than jab back. Personal attacks, even gentle ones, were not her style. I know we both enjoyed it, without ever saying so.

And now I can recall almost none of the words—nothing specific. The things I remember her telling me are so random as to be exasperating. I remember Mom explaining to me the causes of toilet bowl grit (minerals in the water). I remember her teaching me to iron the sleeves and collar of a shirt first. But those beloved bantering sessions have already blurred, leaving behind just the outline of a sharp eye, a keen intelligence, and an animating spirit.

I knew my mother pretty well. Never completely, of course. I wasn't there when the shaping events took place. But I did meet the principal shaper. Her name was Joan too, sometimes called Annie. Annie Slorance was my grandmother. Whatever you might say about Grandma, she was influential. Like gravity on meteors, or meteors on dinosaurs, Grandma made a difference.

The story of my mother's life is largely the story of her relationship with her own mother. The influence was direct at first, but almost as important later. It is a story of struggle, one that my mother almost didn't survive.

Why are some destroyed by flames while others are tempered? My mother's grim determination in the face of increasing paralysis has been further proof of something her children already knew—her character is of steel. Perhaps that's only natural. Grandma was a blast furnace.

4

GRANDMA

UNTIL I WAS twelve, Grandma and Grandpa were a package deal. They visited together—we never saw them apart. They seemed a single entity, like the Beatles.

Then came 1971. The Beatles were long gone. In the very early hours of May 6, we kids were shaken awake and told to get dressed. Jock Slorance, our grandfather, had died of a heart attack. It had not been his first. Perhaps it was an occupational hazard of his chosen trade as a baker, but the cigars couldn't have helped either. Nor did Grandma's habit of making coleslaw with whipping cream. He was seventy-two, though his gravestone wouldn't say so. Grandma fudged the dates to hide the terrible fact that she'd been a year older than her husband.

As the car was being packed Lynn wandered down the street looking up at the stars, angry that the heavens held no sign of the change. I was just sleepy and bewildered, trying to balance the solemnity of the occasion with the excitement of a sudden, starlit journey. We bundled into the Oldsmobile for the long drive to Edmonton. It was my mother's forty-fifth birthday.

At the funeral a piper played, and a kilted man sang "Loch Lomond." It was my first real experience with death. I don't recall coming to any particular conclusions about it.

We kids loved our grandparents. Or so I had thought. In subsequent years I realized what we had all loved about Grandma and Grandpa. It was Grandpa. The two of them had always squabbled, but only in retrospect did I understand the situation well enough to take sides. Grandma, I now understood more clearly, was a giant pain.

I probably picked up on some of this earlier, but when you're still in single digits you don't tend to analyze things that have simply always been. Grandma and Grandpa had always been there, and always honking at each other like a couple of geese in a territorial dispute.

Grandpa was kindly and indulgent with the grandchildren. I loved to watch him shave as he took the implements from a leather kit, whipped up some shaving cream, floated it on the sink water and slapped it on with an old shaving brush, and scraped off the whiskers with a straight razor. He was happy for the audience.

He was different with his wife—prickly and perpetually exasperated, huffing like a steam press. "Motherrrrrr," he would growl to halt some ongoing monologue.

Early in my parents' marriage my father took a train trip with Grandpa through Saskatchewan. Somewhere a few Scotches along the flat, featureless route, the older man spoke of his daughter's good fortune. "I see you and Joan," he said. "It's wonderful the way you are together. You love each other. You talk."

By contrast, the toxicity of our grandparents' relationship could be frightening. "She was extremely hard on

Pop," said my aunt Margaret, the youngest of their three children. "She imposed her will on him."

The poison ran both ways. Margaret recalls an argument when her father slapped her mother—"hard."

Christmas 1969 was our last all together. The highlight was a gift Grandpa received from our cousins. Uncle Stan's three children got him a big trophy, the kind that might be handed out after a high school basketball tournament, with a little plaque inscribed "World's Greatest Grandpa." It was just corny enough to qualify as the best grandpa gift ever. He was completely tickled.

Lynn recalls another gift Grandpa got that Christmas—a pair of socks Grandma had knitted by herself. Grandpa's reaction made Lynn wince. "He opened up the box, looked at the socks, and tossed them aside like a football.

"Grandma wasn't trying to make him miserable. She just was who she was—she couldn't really do anything about it. But he could be quite cruel to her."

Grandma was who she was, all right. I could have been full of sympathy and understanding, had she never come to visit.

MEDUSA WAS NOT born with viper hair. According to the most popular version of the Gorgon legend she was once a fair maiden of many gifts, only later to be transformed into a monster by jealous Athena. And Grandma? We were assured that she had once been young. A formidable lass too. Mom made sure we heard of her youthful accomplishments, when her skill and determination helped rescue her family from poverty back in Scotland. Certainly there was no denying the primal force of the woman. She was will incarnate. You only had to watch her play bridge. It wasn't hard to believe that she had found ways to use her strength in an era when a young woman's options were limited.

But that was ancient mythology to us. The woman we knew was obstinate, willful, capricious, manipulative, and as thoroughly self-involved as a high school prom queen.

Joan "Annie" Barron was born near the border town of Hawick in 1897, one of nine children of Jasper Barron. An estate manager, he lost his position for daring to tell the lord of the manor how his affairs ought to be run. The family was reduced to dirt-floor poverty, not helped by the patriarch's drinking. But if the national beverage had contributed to their domestic predicament, young Annie saw a way out via the national game. She became a scratch golfer. It was a skill she used to form useful social connections, which she then exploited to find new work for her father.

Annie's childhood sweetheart was Jock Slorance of Hawick. No one among their children or grandchildren seems to have ever heard a specific story of how they met. Perhaps they had simply always been aware of each other. Or perhaps by the time there was an audience for the story, it was one they no longer felt the urge to tell.

We heard some non-domestic war stories, though. Jock fought in the Great War and survived that mechanized plague thanks only to a momentary intrusion of humanity. Buried up to the neck by a shell blast in 1918, Slorance came to staring down the barrel of a German rifle. It would have been fairly standard practice at the time for that anonymous soldier to interrupt this delightful family story before it had even begun. But young Slorance was spared. His rewards were dubious—a POW camp, followed by near starvation during a postwar trudge across Germany to Holland, followed by Annie Barron.

Jock Slorance immigrated to Canada. He worked on the Welland Canal and as a cook at a Muskoka Lake resort hotel, where he made batches of pancake batter so large he had to stir them with an oar. Annie joined him, and the couple married in 1923 in Leduc, Alberta. The marriage would last forty-eight years. There were three children—Stan, born in 1924, Joan in 1926, and Margaret in 1927. Eventually they would live to see twelve grandchildren, a narrow plurality of whom would bear the Burgess brand.

Some of the Burgess kids share a weird little trait. It's a little hard to describe. Basically, we have a strong aversion to the sight of bumps. As kids we'd be watching cartoons, and some cat or kangaroo would get hit with a bat a couple of times and we'd shriek. Not because of the violence—it was the little cartoon bumps that popped up on the victim's head. They creeped us out. Near the family cottage at Clear Lake there was a little grove of trees afflicted with a disease that caused the leaves to erupt with bumpy growths. We would stroll through the trees, picking off leaves and compulsively squishing the bumps. Leslie had it worst. It was possible for the other kids to drive her crazy simply by repeating "a cluster of bumps," a phrase that naturally became very popular.

One day Mom admitted that she had grown up with the same odd aversion. "But I was careful never to show it," she insisted.

And really, it wouldn't have been hard to hide. Mom wasn't watching cartoons with us and shrieking along.

It makes for a fascinating case study of nature vs. nurture. Scientific studies of identical twins constantly attempt to discern which traits are inborn and which are learned. If a lab rat may be allowed an opinion about his own experience, I'd argue this shared revulsion, which we called "bump torture," is unlikely to be learned behaviour. I think it is in our genes.

That was surely a disconcerting idea for Mom. The realization that a parent's best efforts cannot prevent certain genetic legacies from being passed along must have led to a few nights staring holes in the bedroom ceiling. Because that was Mom's prime directive all along—to break the chain, to be better than her teacher, to control the inheritance she bequeathed to her children. Our childhoods, she determined, would differ from hers. And she would be a different mother from her own.

Not that she announced this goal every night over dinner to the sound of swelling violins. I don't recall ever hearing her say it. But it was clear that Mom was operating via negative example.

In the airline industry they call it "tombstone technology"—the mechanical and operational improvements that follow a major plane crash. That was Mom's parenting model, more or less—survey the wreckage and vow to do better.

As grandchildren, safely buffered by a layer of management, we did not know exactly what it was like to be raised by Annie Slorance. But we knew enough about our grandmother to shudder at the idea.

You didn't really communicate with Grandma. She communicated with you, and you dealt with it. There was nothing you could give her. Your opinions? Maybe a little advice about recent trends? No. You might as well offer five dollars to a raccoon.

Understanding Grandma was no simple task either. Like learning a language, it was a skill best acquired through early immersion. Mom was the expert. She was our resident Kremlinologist, interpreting for us the mysteries of a strange and frightening regime.

Frequently during Grandma's visits I would overhear a seemingly innocuous exchange that would leave a mysterious chill in the air. It was then necessary to ask Mom to interpret what had just happened. Only she had the internal decoder.

It might start with a remark from Dad: "We need new tires for the station wagon."

To which Mom might reply, "It seems like we just bought the old ones."

Which might then cause Grandma's jaw to clamp like a bear trap and an icy silence to descend. Later, Mom would explain: The issue of tire wear reminded Grandma that the family had left town to drive out east the previous summer, instead of staying home and inviting her to visit. "Aaahhh," we would say.

The first word out of Grandma's mouth was usually, "No." She said it reflexively, like someone else would say, "Well," or "Um," to buy time while formulating an answer. If you said, for example, "They say it could rain today," Grandma might respond with, "No... eh... well... it might rain in the afternoon." That initial "No" was instinctive. It was what she did best, and if upon reflection she found herself forced to agree with something she would then adjust the sentence as best she could.

After Grandpa died we got plenty of Christmas visits from Grandma. It was no accident that her son, Stan, had moved to the New Jersey coast, almost as far from Grandma as was possible to be without needing webbed feet. Margaret was in Ottawa and not putting out the welcome mat. We, however, lived right across the Prairies.

Spending Christmas Eve with Grandma was always going to be a bit like watching Genghis Khan come down the chimney. But there was another aspect to her holiday visits that tended to interfere with the holiday spirit—it was Grandma's tortured relationship with gifts, both given and received. Grandma's philosophy was a sort of twisted tribute to the aphorism "It's the thought that counts." Your thought would be interpreted by Grandma, and the evaluation would be based on both promptness and resale value. Grandma had her very own return policy: If a gift mailed to her did not arrive before her birthday or Christmas, she would send it back. If you cared enough, you would take the trouble to get it there on time.

Even more fraught with import was Grandma's own generosity. She would sometimes slip us kids five-dollar bills—a fortune at a time when we were getting twenty-five-cent allowances. But they always came with conditions. Even then I think we understood that each five was intended to buy us off. Seen in that light, the sum of five dollars took on an insulting significance.

A particularly telling gift was the golf cart. My eldest brother Joe played golf. Grandma decided to show her encouragement of this character-building behaviour with a lavish gift: a two-wheeled bag cart. The gift was sent ahead by special delivery, to be secretly wrapped for Christmas Eve. But the plan went awry. When the box arrived, it was Joe who answered the door. The surprise was ruined. Mom knew the situation held the potential for disaster. "When you open it," Mom instructed Joe, "you really, really have to act surprised."

Christmas Eve came, and Joe opened the box. He gave it his best. "A golf cart!" he enthused. "Wow! Thank you, Grandma!"

From her chair across the room, Grandma watched the performance. Her eyes narrowed; her jaw clenched; her lower lip pushed out. "Och! You knew all along! I wish I'd never bought it!"

Perhaps the greatest of Grandma's mysteries was her love map. Who did Grandma love? More tellingly, who did she dislike? And why?

Not many people were as kind and considerate to Grandma as my father. He listened to her. He was respectful. He was kind. Grandma despised him. Bill Burgess had married her daughter, and some crimes can never be forgiven.

My oldest brother, Joe, born in 1952 would get more of the same. Grandma never warmed to him. The next two kids would fare somewhat better. But enough was enough. At Christmas 1956 my sister Leslie was showing as just a three-month bulge. My grandparents pulled into the driveway; Grandma opened the car door and looked across the yard to where my mother stood waving in the doorway. "Och!" Grandma spat out. "Not again!"

Grandma didn't love many people. But those she loved, she loved like a spider loves flies. Of the five kids her favourite was number three—my brother John, commonly known as Jock. "Shteeve," she once explained, "I love all you kids equally. But... eh... Jock is special."

One day I was sitting in the living room reading when Grandma emerged from her bedroom after an afternoon nap. Catching sight of me, she smiled and began shuffling over. I had plenty of time to wonder what was up. Reaching me, she leaned over and offered her cheek. I planted a dutiful kiss, and she turned to gaze upon me with a blissful smile. Her eyes went wide. "You're not Jock!" she cried. "Och! I thought you were Jock!"

And she tottered away, muttering. In my memory she was wiping her cheek as she went, but that may be a bit of mental embellishment.

As usual, the reasons for Grandma's preference were a mystery. It may simply have been that Jock was named (and nicknamed) after her husband. Jock always doted on Grandma and listened to her with patience and respect. But then so did my father, and Grandma hated him. So who knows?

She also liked Lynn because, in a rare bit of insight, Grandma recognized her willful nature. "You're a little minx," she'd tell Lynn. "You're like me!"

(Later in life this declaration might have hung over Lynn like an oracle's dark prophecy. Eventually George Lucas would come along to explain about the Force and how some go to the Dark Side whereas others use it for good, which must have been a comfort.)

When we were very young, Grandma's favouritism stung. But once the kids got old enough to stop caring, we unloved ones quickly realized our good fortune. Being the object of Grandma's affection meant being snared in her sticky tendrils, subjected to endless, repetitive, solipsistic rambles mixed with stern advice and brandy-fuelled aphorisms. "Eh... life is like a game of golf," she'd say. "You've got to keep trying."

Certain of Grandma's antics inspired only amusement. As she aged, Grandma became increasingly fond of brandy, a fact she was intent on concealing. Her method was to stash brandy bottles in the bedroom closet. She would then go to the kitchen to pour a wholesome glass of ginger ale. A fine plan. Unfortunately Grandma played it badly. "It's only ginger ale," she would loudly proclaim, startling those who would otherwise be reading or watching TV. "I am just going to my bedroom with a glass of ginger ale."

I laughed. And my laughter was not the affectionate kind. I did not see my grandmother as a benign old coot. She was to me a malevolent force, even when not in the house. She could, and did, make my mother cry. My mother would stand silently in the hall, holding the telephone while Grandma detailed some perceived slight or sign of filial ingratitude. By the time Mom finally hung up, there would sometimes be tears in her eyes. I was glad Grandma didn't choose me as one of her pets. It allowed me the luxury of anger and indifference.

Having a kindly grandmother is a wonderful thing. But it's hardly essential. It is not your grandparents who have the power to shape your destiny, to make your home a nurturing, supportive environment or a battlefield of wills. That would be your parents. The old woman, who was just a seasonal annoyance to my siblings and me, was the primary caregiver to my mother. My mother was raised by a woman with a mind like a windowless room, a woman apparently incapable of empathy or self-analysis.

Young Joan would barely make it through that upbringing.

5

THE FOOD CHAIN

BASSANO, Alberta, sits just off the Trans-Canada Highway, eighty-seven miles east of Calgary. It's the kind of lightly rolling prairie country that people claim to hate driving through. Yet show them a photograph of a small combine doggedly wading into vast, yellow canola acres below the wide blue sky with ranks of white cumulus receding to the horizon, and they might just marvel at what a good photographer can make out of nothing.

Those who grow up there need no assistance in seeing its beauty. Bassano is the first place my mother remembers. In 1929, when she was three years old, the Slorance family relocated to Bassano, where Jock would run a bakery.

Joan's earliest memories include her personal picnics—the menu was crackers and water—held in fields of prairie grass, with the crickets and meadowlarks and the unbroken horizon.

One summer day, while driving east on a journey back to Brandon, I see the Bassano turnoff and decide to take it. It's a chance to replace my vague mental picture with first-hand observations, buttressed by a few digital photos. I pass the gas station and the grain terminal, cross the railroad tracks, drive along residential streets with real trees, and quickly reach the little downtown. Unlike many prairie communities, Bassano has more or less held its own. The innovative floating dam opened in 1914 never quite produced the civic boom the town's founding fathers had hoped. But the community maintains a population of roughly 1,400 and shows no signs of withering away like so many other farming centres battling the steady urban migration of the young.

The Imperial Hotel still stands on the wide main street. It's been there as long as the town. These days there's no lobby—the only public entrance is to the saloon. Give or take a few video lottery terminals the room looks as it must have a hundred years ago, and the proof is mounted near the entrance—a seventy-eight-pound sturgeon, pulled out of the Bow River near the Bassano Dam in the year 1913. My grandfather would have seen that sturgeon, but such barroom wonders would have been off limits to the children and womenfolk.

A few old men perch in front of the VLTs. An unsmiling forty-ish woman in a sweatshirt and pulled-back hair wipes the bar and nods at the mention of a bakery. "It used to be across the street," she says.

She's right too. Small towns have long memories. In 1997, British scientists took DNA from a nine-thousand-year-old skeleton found in a cave near Cheddar, England, and traced it to a living relative—a history teacher named Adrian Targett, who lived about half a mile from where the bones were found. Bassano was only founded in 1911, but call back in the year 7873 and someone at the barber-shop will probably know who caught that sturgeon.

There's a Bassano-era photo of our mother and her sister, Margaret, probably six and five years old, dressed in the Highland outfits they wore in local dance competitions. Mom doesn't look happy. But that may simply be because, as the older member of the little troupe, she had to dance the boy's part.

Mom didn't talk too much about her home life. She understood our derisive opinions of Grandma and did not like to fuel the fire. But one story is memorable. When Grandma wanted to punish her children, even over minor issues, they would be sent to the cellar steps. The door would close behind them and they would be left there until they apologized. Young Joan would not apologize. The cellar was pitch black and unheated. "I would sit there forever," Mom told us. Eventually some face-saving truce would have to be brokered by her father, allowing little Joan to emerge from the dark and go to bed. Like her mother, Joan had will—and even at that early age it was bent on defiance.

The Slorance family dynamic was not a simple one. Each of the three children experienced their youth differently. About younger sister Margaret's life and experiences I cannot really speculate; I know that her relationship with her mother was difficult, but how it ultimately shaped her life I do not know. About Stan, I know a little more. Whereas Joan battled her mother and found refuge in her father's affection, her older brother's experience was nearly the reverse.

Stan was a born comedian and prankster who would eventually spend a happy time touring the country in summer stock theatrical productions. Once, when my teenage mother was preparing for one of her first dates,

Stan scattered some of her undergarments around the living room before ushering Joan's suitor into the parlour. "Oh, that Joan," Stan said, picking up a bra. "She just leaves this stuff lying around any old place."

Stan was his mother's favourite—surely a mixed blessing, even then—but suffered under the weight of his father's expectations of what a man should be. Jock Slorance expected toughness, and his preferred seasoning technique was boxing. Stan endured regular beatings from his father, no less painful for being conducted under the Marquis of Queensbury rules. Years later Stan would get a tearful apology from his father. "That was the way we thought things were supposed to done," Jock told his son.

The Bassano Bakery did well for a while. Even the Depression did not seem, at first, a fatal blow—Jock Slorance still managed to open up a new bakeshop and confectionery on Main Street in July 1932. But in this part of the world the worst blows of the Depression were yet to come. The initial crash, and subsequent economic slump, were trouble; still ahead were Biblical plagues of drought, dust storms, hail, and grasshoppers that would spell death for many little towns in southern Alberta. God, it seemed, had lost a bundle on the markets and was throwing a tantrum.

Fire is another popular scourge, one the Almighty often outsources to human agents. Bassano seems to have burned down, a piece at a time, several times over. Meeting halls, hardware stores, vacant shops, the Hunter Hotel, all lighting up in their turn. It had to be discouraging to any spirit of progress. *Gem Theatre Makes Improvements*, reads an August 1928 *Bassano Mail* headline. *New Piano and Up-to-Date Motion Picture Machine Installed*. It is reported that the proprietor hopes soon to be able to show movies continuously without stopping the show to change reels.

All for naught. In 1930 the Gem would burn to the ground. For the next few years the only big popcorn events in Bassano would be fires. They were still a regular source of diversion, though. Reading the archives of the *Bassano Mail* is like reading about the Great Chicago Fire in installments.

Here's one from May 9, 1935: *Fire Destroys Inside of Local Bakeshop; Early Morning Blaze Destroys Oven and Walls of Building—Prompt Action of Fire Brigade Subdues Fire in Hour.*

Early the previous Sunday, the *Mail* reported, one Jas. Snape of nearby Countess was motoring down deserted Main Street and saw the blaze. He awakened proprietor "John Slornace" [*sic*] and raised the alarm. Five hundred feet of hose was laid. The gentle breeze blowing at the time did not spread the fire. The origin of the "configuration" (the reporter perhaps meant "conflagration") had not yet been determined. The oven was rendered unfit for further use; three of the four walls and the ceiling ruined; several hundred pounds of flour ruined. The condition of the molder and mixer still unclear. No other casualties.

There was no insurance. Losing the bakery would be a setback for Bassano as well as the family—for a little town in the thirties, a local bakery was a precious convenience. So other Bassano merchants offered Jock and Annie Slorance no-interest loans to help them rebuild. They did.

But troubles were mounting now. With the Depression deepening, Jock Slorance was supplying bread to grocery stores that could no longer pay their bills. The bakery delivered the bread anyway.

One day Jock reluctantly confronted a grocer whose cheque had bounced. The merchant was sympathetic—in fact, he was outraged at the behaviour of those high-handed bankers. "You mean they didn't cash it?" he fumed. Picking up the telephone, he called the bank. Jock listened as he tore into the manager for the mix-up. "Okay," the grocer told Jock after ringing off, "I straightened it out. Go on back to the bank and they'll take care of it."

Jock took the cheque back to the bank—whereupon he discovered that the merchant's creditors included the phone company. The telephone at the grocery store had not been working for days.

Eventually the Slorance family business fell apart. The bakery was turned over to the government for unpaid taxes. Facing destitution was trouble enough, but the failure must have been particularly hard on a couple whose relationship functioned best as a business partnership. Annie was tough, frugal, and financially shrewd—she had kept the books while Jock handled the baking. It's unlikely they had a lot of romance to fall back on.

Now came one of those rare episodes that we kids would hear about, first-hand from Mom. She would have been about eleven or twelve years old at the time. Her dad, professionally frustrated and personally miserable, decided to leave his wife. Jock Slorance packed his bag, went out the door and down the steps. And then, years before Wayne Newton would turn the same scenario into a maudlin pop song, my mother ran after him and grabbed onto his leg. "Don't leave me," she pleaded.

He turned around. That story is one of the most heartbreaking I know. But then, I knew my grandmother.

Finally Jock found a business partner—a Rosetown, Saskatchewan, café owner with a vacant building suitable for a new bakery. Rosetown would soon become a symbol of better times in the agricultural business, a service centre for some of the most successful farms in the province. Jock Slorance managed to secure a large supply of baker's malt, allowing him to crank out a steady supply of sweet baked goods, much in demand. With the three kids working shifts after school, the bakery business boomed. The financial problems, at least, were over.

Margaret and Stan worked back in the bakery. Joan worked up front in the retail operation, selling bread. "She was very good with customers," Margaret says. "Mother used to say to me, 'Why can't you be more like Joan?'

"A long time later, Joan told me Mother used to ask her, 'Why can't you be more like Margaret?'

Good retail skills aside, there was another reason Joan worked up front: "They thought she was too frail to work in the bakery."

To some extent, the difficulties of my mother's youth must be inferred. She didn't go on about it. We knew what her mother was like. We heard the occasional story of conflict. We knew that being caught up in her parents' corrosive relationship would have been disastrous for a child.

But the main reason we knew my mother had a difficult childhood is that it almost killed her. For years she had been chronically unable to keep food down. At age thirteen Joan weighed less than sixty pounds. Her teeth were being eaten away by stomach acid. She was starving to death. The family doctor declared that without prompt action she would likely be dead within two months.

Annie Slorance was a tough and difficult woman. But her essential nature is a matter of debate.

In his book *The Hero with a Thousand Faces*, Joseph Campbell describes the archetypal tyrant he calls Holdfast. Holdfast lays waste to whatever domain he commands: "This may be no more than his household, his own tortured psyche, or the lives that he blights with the touch of his friendship and assistance."

But, Campbell points out, often it is the hero who becomes the tyrant. The same qualities that allow for effective action are later employed to maintain power and control. What transforms hero into tyrant is the inability to recognize that the situation has changed and that new skills are now needed.

When her family was in crisis back in Hawick, Grandma was heroic. But fierce will and dogged persistence aren't always enough. You can't tackle parenthood like a lion takes down a zebra.

Although I disliked Grandma intensely, I never really thought she had sufficient self-awareness to understand her effect on those around her. Her youngest daughter disagrees. "She knew what she was doing," Margaret told me. "But it didn't matter. She didn't care."

I'm not sure. Grandma seemed to me no more malicious than that hungry lion.

Mom told us the story of coming home after the doctor's dire warning and being taken up to her room. Her mother slipped in to keep watch. "She thought I was asleep. She started crying. It was the only time in my life I ever really heard her cry."

Seriously ill? Saskatchewan circa 1939 would not be the statistician's recommended locale. Yet two factors now worked in Joan's favour. With the family finances on the upswing, there was money. And being the daughter of former amateur golf champ Annie Barron finally moved into the advantage column. A crisis required action, and action she understood. Just point her at a zebra and she was fine. Mother and daughter were soon on a train bound for Minnesota and the Mayo Clinic.

The diagnosis was achalasia—essentially a failure of the esophagus. Her stomach, doctors discovered, had shrunk to the size of a walnut. Mayo Clinic physicians offered two possible explanations for Joan's case. One was prolonged emotional stress. The other was swallowing lye soap.

Shortly thereafter, and for the rest of her life, Annie Slorance would tell the story of how her impish teenage daughter had swallowed lye soap. I am sure she was already convinced of its truth the first time she told it.

Joan underwent immediate force-feeding. "They would feed me every hour," she recalled, "to stretch my stomach. One bite of potato and I would feel full. Then I would have to eat again."

Did young Joan really get achalasia as the result of stress? More than seven decades after that speculative diagnosis, there's no real way of knowing. Even now the reasons for achalasia are not well understood. But achalasia is not anorexia. The results may look similar, but an achalasia sufferer starves for reasons that are strictly mechanical: the consumption apparatus won't function.

Yet when I think of my mother's teenage medical crisis I am reminded of other teens who slowly dwindle away. It has been said of anorexia nervosa patients that they seek control, and calorie intake is the simplest way to exert total control over one's own body.

I don't believe my mother's achalasia represented a subconscious attempt to exert control over her own circumstances. That would be a facile diagnosis, made long after the fact. But the parallels at least are worth noting. My mother was a woman who very much wanted control over her own life. She and her own mother were engaged in a battle of strong wills. Somehow, for young Joan, the result was near starvation.

Joan's physical problem may not have been what we now call an eating disorder. But looking at a mother-daughter struggle like theirs brings to mind a phrase that seems suspiciously appropriate: eat or be eaten.

A network of personal relationships can sometimes resemble a food chain. Not all of us are the dominant predators of our own lives. A child subject to a cruel or domineering parent, or an employee toiling for an unforgiving boss, is forced into a kind of subjugation. She lives the nervous, wary life of a zebra or antelope. All the while her greatest dream is freedom. Not necessarily as a hunter, but perhaps as something like the noble elephant—independent and unafraid.

Even as she struggled to regain control over her own rebellious body, my mother was surely aiming for more. At thirteen years of age she was already looking ahead to the day of escape, freedom, and control. Her goal was not dominance—only autonomy. Joan Slorance struggled and suffered through her youth because she was not cut out for subservience. She needed to be her own master. She needed to escape the tyranny of the food chain.

Meanwhile her medical problem, and its treatment, had several consequences. She got false teeth while still in her teens. She developed a lifelong loathing of feeling full (later to be cursed with a husband who was constantly pestering her to eat from his overstuffed plate). And her swallowing problems never disappeared. In the middle of many family meals she would quietly excuse herself and disappear down the hall to the bathroom to remove a lump of food that had simply stopped in her throat like a lost tourist. Worst of all was when it happened, as it did with reliable frequency, during a restaurant meal or a social outing. For a woman who hated to bring attention to herself, it was a regular trial.

But she rebounded. Slowly the pounds came back. By high school graduation, photographs show an admittedly slight but beautiful young woman.

My grandmother was no cartoon villain. The Minnesota mission showed her talent for decisive action but was by no means the only notation on the good side of her celestial ledger. Back in Bassano in that pre-social-safety-net era, the family had taken in a destitute and abandoned child named Ada. And for all her shortcomings as an emotional provider Annie was at the very least looking after the practical interests of her children in an admirably progressive fashion. For years she had reliably taken her children's bakery wages and socked them away in an education fund. There probably weren't too many students from Rosetown, Saskatchewan, destined for Eastern universities. All three of the Slorance children would go.

In 1944 eighteen-year-old Joan Slorance, a slender redhead with suspiciously good teeth, arrived at Queen's University in Kingston, Ontario. She enrolled in English literature and moved into Ban Righ Hall. She joined the Queen's Highland dancers, a troupe that performed at the football games. Shy, she nonetheless began making friends. One night an outgoing pal named Pat initiated a hairstyle makeover, framing Joan's high forehead with fashionable bangs. In a portrait taken shortly afterward, Joan looks back over her shoulder and smiles. Pat must have smiled too. The bangs worked for Joan. With her mother miles away in Rosetown she probably put on a few useful pounds as well.

I don't imagine Joan ever saw the 1936 musical *Follow the Fleet* with Fred Astaire and Ginger Rogers. A sensible person might be afraid to go to the movies in Bassano, at least not before locating the fire exits. Still, they built the Orpheum a few years after the Gem burned down, so she could have taken it in. If so, she'd have done well to take a few notes. There's a subplot involving Harriet Hilliard (later to become a household name as Harriet Nelson, co-star of *The Adventures of Ozzie and Harriet*). Shy, retiring Harriet is a bit of a wallflower. Then she gets a makeover and attracts the attentions of Randolph Scott, a handsome navy man.

On a campus far from Hollywood, Joan Slorance's sweet-smiling, bangs-bedecked portrait would soon take up residence in the dorm of a besotted young naval officer. Rogers and Astaire they weren't. But they would certainly dance. And, as in any good romance, the plot would take a few hard twists.

6

MADE ON A FRIDAY

I'M PRETTY sure I was made on a Friday.

I don't mean that one day in November 1957 my parents kicked off the weekend by stuffing the existing kids with meatloaf until they were comatose and then pushing the dresser in front of the bedroom door. The scenario behind my conception never was explained to me, thank goodness. Considering the situation—Mom raising four kids with Dad's contribution consisting almost entirely of his meagre United Church minister's salary—one plausible explanation would be liquor. But Mom wasn't a drinker, so the whole project is just hard to fathom. A fifth dependent in a household whose income wasn't even high enough for the family to enjoy the potential tax benefit—not a good idea. If the yardstick is ordinary common sense, my existence is hard to justify.

This implausibility extends to the eventual product. Based on the blueprints, I don't look like a viable concept. In whatever fabrication plant our souls and characters are assembled and bolted I must have represented a serious logistical problem. Parts taken from Dad: garrulous extroversion, an element of showmanship, emotionality, and a certain naïve optimism sometimes shading into outright cluelessness. Mom's contributions: pronounced introversion, shyness, an intensely private nature combined with an inclination toward the analytical and observational. Down on the shop floor it must have been like welding a Hummer to a Prius.

Some vehicles are described as Friday cars. When an expensive new ride begins to limp along like a three-legged mule, while the electrical system springs more surprises than a Japanese game show, it is sometimes said that the car must have been built on a Friday by a workforce already mentally starting their weekends. So it must have been with me. I can only assume that at the crucial moment of my manufacture the five o'clock whistle blew. Saddled with two sets of parts that really should not exist in the same package, the crew slammed me together with some quick soddering and a few hammer blows and headed for the exits.

The results didn't seem promising initially. Scrawny, slightly bluish, sporting a long, ugly red scratch I had apparently given myself in utero, my appearance actually inspired a nurse to say, "Only a mother could love this one."

Happily those mismatched parts turned out to be pretty solid stuff. They put a lot of steel in the fenders back in the day. I have held up pretty well. But it raises the question—how did those parts join up in the first place? What brought Bill Burgess and Joan Slorance together?

The idea that opposites attract is compelling. It fits with the romantic notion of two halves coming together. Most of the anecdotal examples I have encountered suggest that such impulses are best ignored. Whatever urges toward personal completion drive such pairings, they are usually swamped by a flood of annoyance, and relatively quickly. Sexual chemistry hides the issues for a while, and then it's a mixed bobsled run down a fast, winding track. Most of the time it just doesn't work.

There are different kinds of opposites. Some couples differ in temperament while others are opposed in values and world view. My friend Ron's parents were an example of the latter. Ron's dad was a professional hockey player, a locker room roustabout Ron used to call Cowboy. Ron's mom was an early feminist, a misplaced hippie in a Manitoba farming town. By the time I met Ron in elementary school they were already arguing about child support.

My parents were the first type. They tended to share political opinions and saw eye to eye on issues of morality and social justice. But temperamentally they might as well have been Yogi Bear and Ranger Smith. There's almost something perverse about it. Joan Slorance was a young woman whose hatred of being the centre of attention was deep and profound. Bill Burgess was sunny, sweet, gregarious, and, on regular occasions, a human embarrassment generator.

Being a Human Embarrassment Generator (HEG) does not necessarily involve clumsiness or boorish behaviour. What's really required is a complete lack of malice or suspicion. Thinks the HEG: People waiting in grocery store lineups will appreciate the chance to chat with a stranger. Or: If I drink from my soup bowl, people will understand—how can you get to the tasty dregs with only a spoon? Surely people won't judge my character based on large, rainbow-hued food stains on my shirt. That would be crazy. The HEG predicts the reactions of others by the standards of his own benevolent world view.

The Burgess/Slorance pairing shouldn't have worked. Yet contrasting styles and temperaments can also complement. Show business is practically founded on the concept. Nobody ever paid to see a comedy about two roommates who both love a tidy bathroom. Bill and Joan offered each other crucial qualities—a lightening influence and a splash of joie de vivre on one side, a steady hand and some needed guidance and sophistication on the other. Held in common was a natural sincerity—neither possessed the skill or inclination to deceive. Over the years there would be some necessary adjustments. There would be serious rough patches. But mutual respect and the will to communicate were always there. As a result these two people, as different in personal style as a parrot and an owl, would be separated only by death.

They met at Queen's. Joan had already been in Kingston a year when twenty-year-old Bill Burgess showed up. Bill was an Ottawa boy, the son of Joe Burgess, a senior civil servant in charge of the dairy industry. The youngest of eight children, Bill was raised mostly by his older sisters. Bill's mother Lena had died when he was only seven. He came home one day to see her being loaded into an ambulance. He never saw her again, alive or dead—little Billy was considered too young to attend the funeral.

Bill had first attended Queen's in 1943. In 1945 he returned as a young officer fresh from the Royal Canadian Navy. Bill had not seen action. This may be considered his contribution to Allied victory.

By his own admission, Bill was the kind of wet-behind-the-ears young officer regular sailors privately mocked. It was a bit of luck that saw him get his commission at all. In the fall of 1944, as he was on his way into the final oral examination before a panel of admirals and captains, the departing officer candidate muttered, "Carthaginian peace." Thus tipped to the coming question Bill was able to wax on at length about the famous Roman strategy of guaranteeing peace by utterly decimating the homes and fields of their defeated opponent. "The time ran out," he says, "before they could find out how little I knew about guns and munitions and actually running a ship."

He was now a proud probationary sub-lieutenant. A highlight of his brief military career came when he marched a company of trainees straight into a wall. "I called out 'Wheel left' instead of 'Wheel right.' Half of them did it and half didn't. I had to chew the smart ones out for ignoring the order."

History's great events splinter into millions of personal stories. For Bill Burgess and countless other Allied soldiers and sailors, the 1945 debut of nuclear weaponry in Hiroshima and Nagasaki did not represent the fearful dawn of a terrible era. It represented deliverance. "I should have been appalled, but at the time I just thought, 'Great! It's going to be over.'"

In the great tradition of navy life, Bill was walking the deck with a broken heart. He'd been writing impassioned letters to a girl back home. Her name was Mary Lou, the daughter of a well-off businessman. Bill already had some reservations about his lady love. Then the dagger to the heart—friends informed poor, trusting Bill that Mary Lou was really doing her bit for the war effort. "They said she was chasing after anything in a uniform."

One day Bill was the lone duty officer on board HMCS *Lanark* in Liverpool, Nova Scotia, when a message arrived. A quick discharge was available to the first officer who could provide evidence of acceptance at a college. Briefly abandoning his post, Bill ran to the telegraph office and sent a telegram to Queen's, where he had spent a term two years earlier. His acceptance arrived the next day. Dad and the navy were quits.

The old song instructs: One must be a football hero to make it with the beautiful girls. The assumption is that one ought to be a star. Bill Burgess was a decent lineman on a mediocre Queen's Golden Gaels team. "We got beat about 65–10 once," Bill says. "Guys were a little pissed off about them running up the score."

A college football team is a travelling road show. The Queen's team was accompanied by cheerleaders, a pipe band, and Highland dancers. Like the players, the performers needed to run through their paces. So at practice time the team, band, and dancers would all be at the field together. It was at one of those practices that Lineman Bill chased a stray ball that had rolled close to where the pipe band and Highland dancers were standing. Among the dancers in their comely kilts, one in particular stood out.

Later Bill quizzed friends: "Does anybody know that red-headed Highland dancer?"

"I know her," said his friend Marvin. "In fact I've got a date with her the weekend we go to McGill."

That weekend attack on Montreal would be a success on many levels. It began with a truly impressive bit of psychological warfare waged by the Kingston visitors.

The night before the game three squadrons of cars were mobilized. Each squad carried a different colour of paint. Red cars, gold cars, and blue cars left for the McGill campus in staggered shifts. "A lot of the guys in the student body that year were fresh out of the military," Dad says. "They were used to running precision operations."

By the time fans began arriving for the Saturday contest the football stadium had been repainted in the official colours of Queen's, right down to the fire hydrants. The Golden Gaels went on to win the game.

That night a smaller operation prepared to deploy. Marvin, a true wingman, was perfectly happy to set it up. First he called an old girlfriend to play the role of Bill's companion on a double date. Early in the evening, the switchover was effected. Marvin and his old flame paired up, leaving Bill and Joan together at a hot Montreal jazz club. "I guess it wasn't Oscar Peterson," Bill says, "but it was somebody good."

On Sunday Joan was coaxed by her best friend Marie to visit a Montreal printing shop. At some point during the big date, Bill had made a chance remark about how football linemen never get the headlines. Thus when the Queen's contingent boarded the train for the ride home, a special edition was circulating, complete with banner headline—*"Queen's Victorious; Burgess Stars!"*

One day soon afterward Joan and Marie rode their bicycles down Bill's street and were invited up for coffee. The train of romance was tooting its happy horn. "Right away, we found out we could really dance," Dad says.

There are black and white photos from that year. Seen from the far side of over a half a century's worth of domestic struggle, the pictures are startling. There are a number of shots with Bill in his navy greatcoat and Joan in a fur coat. One shows a laughing Bill holding Joan aloft. They are a traffic-stopping pair. Dad with his wavy black hair, clean jawline, and happy grin, Mom with her long red hair, shy smile, and sylph-like frame—it could have been a shot of Ronald Reagan and Jane Wyman, horsing around after a long day on the set.

Did they see themselves that way? Doubtful. When Dad looks at Queen's pictures, he often cringes at the clothes he was wearing. Despite being the city boy of the pair, he felt himself unsophisticated. How unsophisticated? Once during a road trip with some football buddies, he innocently asked, "What's that white line on the road for?"

"They couldn't believe it," he recalls with a wince. This spectacular ignorance of motoring knowledge was traceable to his father. A nineteenth-century man, Joe

Burgess was already in his thirties when automobiles began frightening the horses. "He never owned a car," Dad says. "Couldn't see the point of wasting a couple of thousand dollars when you could just as easily take the streetcar." (Ahead of his time, really.)

Bill Burgess must have cut quite a figure in 1945—a tall navy veteran in full sub-lieutenant's regalia. But for proud young sons, ego adjustments are always close at hand. "After I got my officer's commission I went to some reception with my dad. I was wearing my naval uniform, proud as a peacock. And then Dad introduced me to some people: 'Have you met my son, Billy?' I was mortified."

Nor was he well suited to the role of smooth young swain dressed in navy whites. "I used to go on and on to Joan about history," he says. "I'd talk about the 'Ten Reasons for Confederation,' and stuff like that."

As I say, he really was good-looking.

Or perhaps Joan was simply drawn to a man so unself-conscious that he would sweet-talk his lady love with detailed accounts of nineteenth-century politics. She remained painfully shy. Joan always envied the gregarious nature and social ease displayed by Margaret, who was both more social and more voluptuous: "Margaret was always very outgoing and popular. She just seemed to fit in easily."

Mom did have other suitors, though. There was one named Roy, and another named Walter. We knew of the latter because Mom later reminisced about how she and her roommate Marie would serenade each other in trilling falsetto: "Walter, Walter, leeeeaaaad me to the altar..."

Walter would find himself left at the curb. Bill and Joan's first kiss was accomplished while she sat perched on the bar of his bicycle. "I managed to sort of nuzzle her neck as I pedalled along. And we kissed."

Things were pedalling along quickly.

At Christmas 1945 Joan came out to Ottawa and met Bill's father. Joe Burgess was impressed. Unlike others in the house, Joan would get up early enough to help him make breakfast. Bill took Joan out skiing to Ottawa's Dome Hill, filled with romantic dreams: "I had visions of us skiing off into the future together."

Joan would never put on skis again. As for their glorious future, there was a major face plant coming just over the next hill.

One afternoon in Kingston Bill had a date with Joan's sister. It was okay, though. Margaret was helping him pick out a ring. "I thought they were a wonderful couple," Margaret says. "They were very good together."

The blissful Queen's term came to its April conclusion. Joan Slorance returned to Rosetown, engagement ring on her finger. Her mother was waiting.

What Annie Slorance expected from her daughters' university experiences can only be guessed. But it's unlikely she envisioned them with fulfilling professional lives. Rosie the Riveter had had her moment, but the war was over and now the world was scheduled to resume its normal course. Men would pursue careers—as doctors or lawyers, if they hoped to impress Annie Slorance— whereas women would revert to the usual supporting roles.

Bill Burgess had plans to be a teacher. His family had urged him to take up medicine, but a young history buff with a squeamish streak is no budding Dr. Kildare. Strike one. A summer visit to Rosetown didn't help. It was Grandma's first look at him. "I had been working on a road crew earlier that summer. And my clothes— you know, I didn't have anybody giving me advice about that."

Strike two. Grandma likely threw in the third strike free.

Grandma was too clever to throw a fit. Instead she sought to offer her impulsive middle child some constructive advice. "If Bill is planning to stay in school he'll need your help," Grandma reasoned. "While he studies and gets established he might need you to do secretarial work. Why not stay here and take stenography classes? It will be more practical than going back to Kingston."

Taking her mother's advice, Joan would not return to Queen's in the fall of 1946. She and Bill would be separated by a couple of thousand miles—more than enough room for Grandma to bring her game.

As the summer of 1946 came to an end things still seemed to be going well. Bill was preparing to leave Rosetown for the next term at Queen's, and a September 2 outing generated a photo record. There are numerous sultry snapshots of twenty-year-old Joan. Tellingly, each carries a self-deprecating remark on the back. "Where did I get that stupid grin?" she writes on one perfectly lovely shot. Another is captioned: "The mouth reminds me of Martha Raye" (the popular singer and actress whose nickname was "Big Mouth"). A third is more teasing: "Windblown—I guess that's okay by you." There's a photo of a reed-slim Bill, swinging a golf club. "What style!" she writes. "What a man!"

What happened next can be assumed, if not precisely known. A young couple, now thousands of miles apart, one immersed in school, the other isolated in rural Saskatchewan. And Annie Slorance, that assiduous planter, cultivating her garden of weeds.

For a while things seem okay. Joan kept a scrapbook of campus newspaper clippings, faithfully mailed by Bill. Postcards depicting Queen's were carefully pasted in. At the very least, she was missing the idyllic campus life.

By the end of '46 the scrapbook peters out. One day,

when Kingston was in the grip of winter, Bill received a package. Inside was Joan's engagement ring.

He promptly lost it. "I put it in a drawer at my father's house. I think one of my nieces must have pulled it out. It just disappeared."

Bill's career path now changed abruptly. "I was completely in the depths at that point," he says. "I turned to Psalm 23 ('The Lord is my Shepherd, I shall not want...'). It was the only part of the Bible I really knew, and it offered some support. It was the first time the Bible had become personal to me. God became real.

"I realized later that it also connected me to my father. When I was a very young boy we would go to church together. I was the youngest and I was the only one who went with him. Dad would travel for months at a time—those Sundays were about the only time I had him to myself. I would sit beside him and look around the church and daydream. It was the closest to him I could be."

So in the fall of 1946 Bill Burgess was no longer engaged and no longer bound for a classroom career. He was now a heartsick young lover and a candidate for the ministry.

Not that he had given up on romance. "I kept writing to Joan. I was careful about how I signed them. I wrote 'Yours sincerely' on the bottom of one, or 'Affectionately yours.' I think I was probably trying to be sarcastic."

The letters would continue for more than two years. There was one awkward Edmonton visit. But their status remained quo.

There were other women. While serving as a student minister on little St. Joseph Island on Lake Huron, Bill fell into a relationship with a woman named Madge. By that time he was no longer regaling sweethearts with tales of Canadian political history. He talked about his old girlfriend instead. "I was always talking about Joan," he says. "Maybe as a bit of an excuse."

Poor Madge heard so much about the mysterious, perfect, saintly Joan that she decided to investigate. On a summer trip to Alberta Madge called her up for a lunch date. Back on St. Joe's Island come fall Madge was sullen. "You know," she told Bill, "she's just a woman. Just an ordinary woman."

Bill thought otherwise. But for once, he kept his mouth shut.

He kept writing to Joan, awaiting developments. It was a tricky situation. You can't wish unhappiness on a woman you still care about. But neither do you want her to prosper without you. Bill could not know it from her polite letters, but in fact his former fiancée was not doing well at all.

By 1947 the Rosetown bakery had been sold to a former employee. Jock Slorance had experienced a remarkable turnaround—from relinquishing a failed business to comfortable retirement in about eight years. (After the sale the Rosetown bakery would burn to the ground, reportedly struck by lightning. Grandpa always suspected that if lightning actually was involved it probably ignited a healthy sprinkling of kerosene.)

The Slorance family moved to Edmonton, the (relatively) bustling Alberta capital, and bought the house at 12008 96th Street. Their new family doctor was quick to get to know them. His response when Joan came for an appointment early in '49 suggests that he had come to understand the family dynamic rather well. "You need to get away from your mother," he told Joan. "If you want to go back to school, I think it would be a good idea. But whatever the reason, you need to get out."

Joan conveyed to her parents an edited version of the doctor's advice. Grandma respected doctors. "Going back to Queen's is a good idea," she said. "We'll come with you."

Grandma promptly arranged the rental of a spacious Kingston apartment. With the other two Slorance kids already gone from Queen's, it would just be the three of them. Joan's new college roommates would be her mother and father. But at least she was coming back.

By that time Bill had left poor Madge and St. Joe's Island behind, moving on to his latest pastoral assignment. He received Joan's news while in the southeast Saskatchewan village of Handsworth.

Want further information about Handsworth? Google it. If nothing else, you will discover an object lesson in web marketing software. Matchmaker.com offers this automated response: "Handsworth dating for the Handsworth single. Meet thousands of Handsworth singles through one of the best Handsworth online dating sites!"

This is both socially and mathematically impossible. Handsworth is now officially classified in Saskatchewan census records as a ghost town.

There were still a few Handsworthians above ground in 1948 when Bill arrived. Thirty-eight, to be precise. "I was number thirty-nine."

"I see you voted for Tommy Douglas in the provincial election," one local told Bill. Since everyone knew exactly how everyone else in town voted, it wasn't hard to spot the new ballot. Handsworth was the kind of town where a person could scan the shelves at the general store and figure out what the new student minister had bought for lunch.

One day he drove the church's old Model A Ford to the village post office. A letter from Joan was waiting. "I couldn't wait to read it so I opened it as I was driving home. When I read that she was coming back to Queen's, I drove straight into the ditch."

None of the thirty-eight potential victims was struck.

Nonetheless, the population of Handsworth soon declined by one—a trend that would prove ominous.

That fall Joan and her parents drove across the country to Kingston. If she had looked bad before, that family trek was no help.

For years Bill had been mooning over his framed portrait of Joan smiling back over her shoulder, her lovely, gentle face framed by her new bangs. When he next caught sight of her, Joan was standing in line to register for the Queen's fall semester. "She was emaciated and pale," he says. "She really looked awful."

Nonetheless, she was soon back into the campus fling. Joan rejoined the pipe band as a Highland dancer. Bill was still a Golden Gaels lineman. That year the big fall game was in Toronto. Bill made sure that he had a seat on the train that would carry the pipers and dancers on the three-hour journey back to Kingston. "That train trip did it," Bill says. "When we got home we took a long walk in Macdonald Park. I walked her home and, for the first time in a very long time, I kissed her."

Bill Burgess and Joan Slorance were back together.

Then Bill immediately tried to screw it up. His sincere good intentions, obvious by now, were not exactly wedded to a keen sensitivity. "I didn't phone her for a whole week after that. There was football practice and a lot of course work. By the time I called she was so mad she didn't want to speak to me."

This crisis would be thankfully brief. Surely Joan couldn't stay mad at Bill. Anybody who wasn't her mother could see his essential character. He was as good-natured as a cartoon rabbit.

They would be married in Edmonton on December 28, 1950, during Christmas break. Photos taken at the reception suggest it was a good time. That's nice. It wouldn't last.

7

A BUMPY RIDE

WHEN I was about eleven, I remember telling a friend: "I know my Mom isn't beautiful."

The statement was made with apparent conviction. But in truth it was just a searching attempt to come to grips with that age-old problem: Is my mother a woman like other women? What sort of woman is she, compared with others? Could my mother truly be a sexual being?

Looking at old photographs now, it's clear I was an ignorant Philistine. Mom exhibited a clear and confident sense of style, when she was given the chance to dress up a little. But in my defence she rarely got that chance, at least when we were kids. And her brand of quiet taste was not the kind an oblivious young lad would perceive anyway.

Perhaps I thought beautiful meant Marilyn Monroe. Mom was a little more Shirley MacLaine, if Shirley had spent eleven hours a day chasing a gang of hyperactive juveniles in between bouts of scullery work. Mom could never be called hard-looking, but neither was she soft. Her mouth often had a grim set, and she was not quick to smile. She wasn't curvy—never had the spare poundage for that. For all the times we went to the beach I recall seeing her in a bathing suit once. Mom took to water like a cat.

Perhaps my opinion was a reflection of Mom's general demeanour. She was no giggling flirt. Nor was she the romantic of the family firm. That, for sure, was Dad. If there was a sentimental tale to be told of their courtship or early married life it came from Dad—and it usually wouldn't get far. Like a cheerleader at a chess match, Dad would find he wasn't getting a lot of support from the gallery. Mom would get a sort of dryly withering look before bringing up some detail Dad had omitted—some telling point that cast a new light on the story and left poor Dad looking like a puppy whose gaze has just been directed to a new carpet stain. There were plenty of carpet stains to point to. This was a man who had showed disapproval of his bride's wedding gown.

"I didn't mean to," Dad explained, frequently. "I was just shocked. I must have had this look on my face."

Must have. It was definitely noted by its target, a bride who was being punished for being slightly ahead of her time. Joan was in fact wearing a very stylish dress—not quite ankle-length with no train. Very modern. As it turned out, too hip for the room.

We got pictures of that dress, although just barely. No one ever got around to making copies of the official wedding photos. The only pics in the family album have "Proof" stamped on them. The lost engagement ring, the stunned wedding gown reaction, the never-ordered photos—there is hanging about the entire Burgess-Slorance wedding a whiff of disaster.

The couple was married at Robertson United Church in Edmonton. The groom was twenty-five, the bride twenty-four—a mature couple by the standards of the time. The resumption of classes at Queen's precluded any immediate honeymoon. They would take a train back to Ottawa to visit with Bill's family, arriving New Year's Day. Here again, trouble.

Bill and Joan caught a train from Edmonton down to Calgary, where they would pick up the main line headed east. But their train was cancelled. The railroad made arrangements for the newlyweds to get home on the only transport available—a troop train. Joan Burgess, née Slorance, would be the only woman on board.

Their sleeping quarters were open for all to see, and many did—our brave boys in uniform, filing past to leer at the only double-X chromosome on board. Finally, a kindly porter put up a curtain to protect their privacy. Shortly afterward the conductor took it down. "You didn't pay for that," he explained.

And so the peep show went on until Ottawa. "I was on the top bunk reading *Great Expectations*," Dad recalls. "I could hear Joan crying softly in her bunk. When you're newlyweds and your bride is crying, you know it's not going well."

They were met in Ottawa by some of Bill's old buddies, none of whom Joan knew. Afterward she still didn't know them sober. It was after all early on New Year's Day. At the Burgess family home, the couple was installed in Bill's old room—altered circumstances that did not escape the attention of a sharp young niece. "Who's that sleeping with Uncle Bill?" the little girl yelled down the stairs.

Several days into the new enterprise, and so far not a single warm and fuzzy tale destined to delight future generations.

Their first flat in Kingston seemed decent enough, until Joan discovered the lack of running water. Water had to be hauled to the kitchen from the bathroom down the hall, which was shared with the landlady. Here were all the character-building qualities of pioneer life, with the advantages of the city—including entertainment. Home alone one day, Joan was startled by strange noises. They seemed to be coming from the basement—a cacophony of shouting and percussion pouring out the floor vents. The landlady's son was using the place to hold regular revival meetings.

Joan wouldn't be home alone for long. Almost immediately after returning to Queen's, Bill realized something was wrong. He could hardly climb the staircase. "Of course my classmates were all bugging me. 'Look at that—married two weeks and can't even make it up the stairs. Ain't love grand?'"

It wasn't love. It was rheumatic fever. Bill would not be the first groom to spend his first month of wedded bliss in bed, weak as a kitten. Joan would not be the first young bride to be asked to play nurse. But it's supposed to be more fun.

Those may still have been happy times. Anecdotal evidence from other newlyweds suggests that troubles are more easily borne at that novel and exciting early stage of domestic life. Dad certainly remembers the period fondly. But that's the tricky thing about early Burgess family stories—coming from Dad they are happy. Mom's state of mind is always harder to determine.

She'd come through a lot of changes, quickly. She had gone to Queen's as a prospective business student and discovered instead a love of English literature; pulled back into her mother's orbit she had finally returned to Queen's and rekindled a lost love. Now she was the young bride of a soon-to-be-ordained United Church minister.

Perhaps Mom's later stories of that time were coloured by her retroactive knowledge of what was coming—life as a small-town minister's wife and a new role as a human production line with an output that would shame Henry Ford. The academic life would soon seem very far away.

In 1951 the Reverend Bill Burgess received his first pastoral charge as an ordained minister. Chicago and New York were apparently unavailable. He got Stoughton, a town of roughly half a thousand souls in the southeastern quadrant of Saskatchewan.

Stoughton in the 1950s was the picture of a bygone age—the wide main street with its tidy little storefronts, grain elevators, fields of golden wheat, and key parties.

Later immortalized in the book and film *The Ice Storm,* both set in 1970s America, key parties involve groups of married couples who throw their keys into a bowl. Keys are fished out at random to create new couples, who then repair to private bedrooms. In little Stoughton, five years before the publication of *Peyton Place,* and with the seventies still a far-off vision of space-age jumpsuits and flying cars, folks were apparently rather ahead of their time. "The doctor who lived across the street with his lovely wife was involved," Dad said later. "I think I briefly considered preaching a sermon about it."

Stoughton key parties must have suffered obvious disadvantages when compared with similar gatherings in, say, Indianapolis. The population at the time could not have been much more than five hundred. Subtract the kids, the old, and the happily incurious, and you are not left with much of a talent pool. It is arguably one of the perks of being the local minister that you would get no invitations to such events.

Shortly after the young marrieds set up house, Bill's father, Joe, and sister Belle paid a visit. As a senior bureaucrat in charge of dairy production, Joe Burgess was like a king moving among his subjects. He was eager to visit a nearby farm. On arrival they were greeted with a pan of disinfectant—there had been a local outbreak of hoof-and-mouth disease. Joe Burgess stepped out of the pan, shook the drops of disinfectant from his boots, and muttered to his son: "They sure are suspicious of government people out here."

As for Belle, she toured the family home and summed up the locale with a realtor's eye. "Every window I look out," she said, "there's an outhouse."

Small farming towns are close-knit places. Paradise lost, according to Thornton Wilder and John Mellencamp. Hell, if you have the wrong neighbours. There is a point at which neighbourly concern crosses the line into outright criminality. The Burgess family lived next door to a woman named Maude. Maude headed the manse committee, which oversaw matters concerning the house the Burgesses now occupied with their first child, little Joey, born in 1952.

United Church ministers' families lived in church-supplied housing—an important perk considering the modest salary, but in practice rather like the experience of poor orphans living on the charity of rich relatives. The manse committee had jurisdiction over all decisions concerning the house, even down to Joan's request to purchase a cover for a ratty old couch (denied). Maudey took her responsibilities seriously.

This is how seriously: Once when Bill and Joan went on vacation, Maude took the liberty of letting herself into the manse. There she found that new linoleum had recently been laid in the kitchen. To Maudey, it was an abomination. An exorcism was required—the Protestant kind. Maude cast out the new linoleum and replaced it with a variety more to her liking. And so the kitchen was cleansed and made whole. No thanks necessary. Maude was just doing her job.

A measure of vengeance would eventually come—served up small-town style, all white and fluffy. For local women the social yardsticks of that time and place were domestic, a series of deceptively competitive displays of household competence. The brightest victory flags of all were the flapping lines of wash hung out on the line Monday morning—clean, fresh, and best of all, first. Monday was wash day, just as surely as Sunday was the sacred Sabbath when no work could be done. Battle was not to be joined until Monday. The woman whose laundry appeared first on Monday morning was clearly a Stoughton Floyd Patterson, a household heavyweight champ. That tended to be Maude. It sure wasn't Mom.

A small-town minister's spouse is the local Caesar's Wife, expected to be a shining example of all things good and decent. Joan did possess some useful traits for the role—she was quiet and circumspect. But it was a role she never felt up to. A new mother, intensely private, uncomfortably analytical, and lacking in glib self-confidence, she was unsure of the domestic skills she knew would be the basis of her reputation with many townsfolk. Her strong points must have seemed as useless as good penmanship in a fist fight. And every Monday morning she had Maude's wash slapping her in the face, a weekly reminder of her own perceived shortcomings as a housekeeper.

One Sunday night on his way back from the church Dad decided to hop the backyard fence, intending to check in with Maude and her husband about some manse-related issue. Looking through the back screen door, he caught sight of Maude's husband. He was busy separating and soaking the laundry, getting a head start on tomorrow's assault. On the sacred Sabbath, no less. "It's the minister!" Maude shrieked.

Too late. Busted. Talk about dirty laundry—Old Maude was a washday cheat. The stain of sin was on her queen-size sheets and sensible undergarments. The tale of her downfall would become a revered chapter in the Burgess oral history.

BY 1954 LYNN had been born. Bill's father died that year, shortly after his youngest son made it back to Ottawa to see him one last time. "I came into the hospital room, and he asked me to read the sports section to him," Dad said. None of the five kids would have personal memories of Grandpa Joe.

The growing Burgess family moved twenty-five miles away to Fillmore, Saskatchewan, there to grow some more. Brother Jock was born in '55. Three kids now. Although one day, it went back to two.

"Dad ministered to all the churches in the area so we knew all the farmers," Joe says. "I was probably four—I think this was the summer of 1957. We were at a picnic at a prairie lake near Fillmore. I had to take a dump. Dad told me to go to the outhouse. Between where we were and the outhouse was this major cloud of mosquitoes. It seemed to me that he was trying to kill me."

Joe went about halfway and stopped, dropping his shorts in the open air. There was no escaping the steaming evidence of his disobedience. "The only thing to do now," he recalls, "was run.

"I ran behind a parked car and peered around at the group. Then to the next car. Then out to the road. We were in the country, so all the roads were straight, intersected by other roads in a patchwork system that connected all the farms. I set out. Eventually I came to a crossroad and turned right. I trudged along and after a while I started to cry—but what choice did I have? The sun was going down, so it was late—I had been gone four or five hours at least. There was a farm coming up on my left and I had decided that I was going to spend the night under a big tree in the front yard. Then I saw this car racing up a side road, and then another came over a rise behind me. They had seen my footprints in the dirt, and were following them.

"I will always remember Mom's face when they brought me back and put me in her arms—red and streaked from crying. She was sobbing. She just held on to me so tight. I don't have any memory of being punished.

"I heard later," Joe says, "that they had been getting ready to drag the lake."

Leslie was born in 1957. It was this fourth baby bulge that drew Grandma's infamous epithet, spat out in the driveway: "Not again!"

Mom would always describe this as the most difficult of her five pregnancies. It was not planned. She was stressed and sick. "Mom used to actually lose weight after a pregnancy," Lynn says. "She gained less weight than the baby and fluid weighed, so she ended up weighing less afterward than she had at the outset. We sucked every bit of fat out of her body."

Joan knew the pregnancy would be unpopular with her mother, and added to the pressure of Grandma's disapproval was the knowledge that the already-strained family finances would now be stretched like gum on a hot sidewalk. She felt it was only responsible to consider the options.

In her doctor's office she explained the circumstances, reviewed the arguments. He asked her a simple question: "What do *you* want to do?"

"I want to have the baby," she said.

There are many battles in a war for independence. Perhaps final victory can never be declared. But this one was big. Telling the story later, Mom would say, "All the stress and uncertainty went away. It all became clear as soon as I answered."

So clear in fact that she was not even displeased when it all happened again the following year. Not even when the nurse took one look at scrawny, scratchy Baby Number Five and announced, "Only a mother could love this one."

She did. I never had a moment's doubt about that. Although they wisely kept me away from mirrors in the early years.

Born without physical beauty, I did possess a quality my siblings lacked—the constitutional right to become president of the United States. A month before my birth the family had taken up residence in Collins, Ohio, while Dad pursued a master's degree at the Oberlin Graduate School of Theology. I was born a Canadian Yankee in the Fisher-Titus Hospital in Norwalk, Ohio. In that preenvironmentalism era, the town was often described as sitting just outside the smell of Lake Erie. Norwalk would later lend its name to the renowned virus, popular on cruise ships. I imagine there's a sign as you drive in.

The family was now complete. Mom made sure of that. Someone at Fisher-Titus had told her about an operation for men, and Dad dutifully checked in the very next week. I would be the last happy accident ever to get a meal ticket at the Burgess house.

Collins was tiny. The Burgess bloc alone had the electoral muscle to take over the mayor's office, had it not been for our eligibility issues. Dad put himself through school serving as minister in the local Methodist church, working on his degree during the week. "I think I was so focused on what I had to do for school that I didn't really stop to think about the job Joan was doing," he said later.

Others were keeping a closer watch. Neighbours Bob and Martha lived about a hundred yards up the street, with a clear view of our big, red, cedar-shingled church manse. One summer night Martha saw the lights burning late at Casa Burgess and knew that, whatever was going on, it was preventing poor young Joan from a good night's sleep. Next morning she showed up at the door and announced she was taking the older kids to the county fair in Norwalk. Not every small town was claustrophobic; not every neighbour was Maude.

One winter night another neighbour named Ross, paying an after-dinner call, was stunned to see eighteen-month-old Leslie being put to bed wearing a snowsuit. It was a necessity, Joan explained—the old mansion was heated by an antique coal furnace that blew all its heat through a single large vent, located at the base of the stairs. If the vent represented our sun, the upstairs bedrooms would be Saturn, Neptune, and Pluto.

At the next meeting of the church volunteers committee Ross got busy knocking heads together. Renovations commenced shortly.

Our neighbours on one side were Jim and Audrey, until their house burned down. Even as fireman were chopping holes in the roof, Audrey was in our kitchen, hysterical. "The firemen are going upstairs," she told Mom. "The beds aren't made! I didn't get the chance to clean!"

Paramedics gave her a tranquilizer shot.

Just then the school bus turned into the street. Five-year-old Lynn was arriving home. Seeing the blazing house, she rushed to the front of the bus. "Stop!" she told the driver. "Let me off! I'm a member of the Smokey the Bear Club!"

It was true. Mom had allowed her to join that august society for kids who wish to prevent forest fires. The circumstances here were not precisely as specified in club rules—no bears were in peril—but it was a genuine five-star conflagration. And that's what all the weeks of instruction are about. "The driver let me off too," Lynn says.

Not surprising. This was Little Grandma in action, a fearsome force even in miniature. And the yards were huge on our street, so stopping at the neighbour's house meant dropping the bossy little tyke quite a long way from home. However, this potentially heroic intervention would be thwarted. "Mom wouldn't let me go help. I was mad. What is the point of being in the Smokey the Bear Club if you're not allowed to fight fires?"

Our American Dream lasted only a couple of years. In 1960 the first American advisors were already in Vietnam, and I had that American birth certificate. No doubt sensing the return of the draft, I was anxious to get my diapered ass back to Canada. Luckily Dad now had his degree and a posting back in Saskatchewan, at the Regina field office of the United Church.

8

REGINA

REGINA TAKES a lot of knocks. "Flat as pee on a plate," my friend Tom says. Never once described as the Paris of the Prairies. Jann Arden once called it "the town that rhymes with fun." Locals say you can watch your dog run away for a week.

But a hometown is like a religion. Get it into a child's head early and you bypass the critical faculties. Sights seen with young eyes will always hold special wonder. Let New York sophisticates sneer how they will—four out of five Burgess kids considered Regina a land of enchantment. At least 50 percent of our parents felt the same.

We would spend five years there—formative years, and not just for Burgesses. When we arrived John F. Kennedy was still a presidential candidate, and for the first few years the radio played Frank and Dean and a lot of guys named Bobby. By the time we left Saskatchewan the province had become a test case for socialized medicine, U.S. Marines had landed in Da Nang, and at least one of the kids owned a Beatle wig.

Our salmon-pink bungalow sat on a street full of young families, out near the edge of town. Joe's Confectionery was at the end of the block. A block or two beyond that the sidewalk stopped abruptly, and you stepped off into open prairie. As our mother had done in 1930s Bassano, we were free to roam the plains. Pack a little lunch, stop in at Joe's for a two-cent paper bag of assorted candy—sugar peanuts, Scotch mints, caramels— and you were on safari. Grasslands, hillocks, gullies, and trees, though not too many of the last—just enough to provide the occasional shady oasis, not enough to crowd or oppress or interfere with the high, white-flecked sky.

Brown-and-white buses shaped like loaves of bread motored past our house, trailing blue fog. Nothing takes me back to that time like the smell of diesel fumes. Our street was lined with Chevy Bel Airs, Ford Falcons, and AMC Ramblers, two-tone beauties with chrome and plush and nary a buckle or harness to prevent your sudden launch through the windshield and onto the hood. Let Ralph Nader complain all he likes—at least by that time hood ornaments were being phased out, which made for safer landings.

We lived at 5320 Second Avenue. Sing it! We did. Mom and Dad made a little jingle out of our home address so we'd remember it if we ever got lost, or if our parents ever tried to abandon us at a public swimming pool and sneak away. But to be fair, that only happened once.

It was an honest mistake, they insist. Certainly there was no shortage of us, and small details can be easy to miss. The evidence is in the family photo albums. Other kids got individual snapshots. But after a while the novelty wears off, and film is expensive. Me? I'm in a few crowd scenes.

So one day, when I was three or four years old, the family was at the local public swimming pool. The hour got late. I must have dawdled while everyone else was piling into the car. The result formed one of my earliest memories: watching the tear-drop tail lights on our burgundy Chevy station wagon recede down the street as I stood on the sidewalk, dripping.

Cool in a crisis, I went straight to a security guard and announced myself as a lost boy. I knew our phone number and sang our address. "What's your name?" the man asked as he dialled.

"William," I replied.

This was technically correct. William is in fact my first name, though everyone called me by my second. As a young man Dad had always loathed being called "Billy," and didn't want the same for his own son. So I became Steve. But now I was dealing with a man in uniform, and it seemed to me formality was called for. My first name was more official, and that's the one I gave.

Thus the unfortunate moment when Dad answered the phone and the security guard asked whether he had a son named William. "No," said Dad. "No, I don't."

Suddenly it began to look like this abandonment had been no accident. The guard looked at me, perhaps wondering what my little game might be. I didn't know what else to tell him.

Happily, before hanging up Dad took the opportunity to count noses. Panic ensued. The Bel Air belched fire as I was hurriedly retrieved. Stammered explanations were offered to pool staff. I don't recall whether we ever went back—it's likely that our photos were posted on the security office wall just in case.

In 1960 the five Burgess children ranged in age from seven years to eighteen months. That roiling mass of tadpoles was hard enough to manage even when two were watching. Most of the time it was only Mom. Dad's duties at the United Church field office meant a lot of travel, training, and seminars. There was very little spare money for babysitters.

It helped some that we were easily bribed. Since Mom was forced to take us all along on shopping trips to the White Rose supermarket, she would lay down the rules beforehand: "If everyone behaves, you get animal crackers."

Powerful incentive in those straitened times. A family friend recalls: "You kids all followed behind like baby ducks." For crackers. We were non-union.

Animal-shaped perks were not always sufficient. The prevailing attitude toward corporal punishment was different in the early sixties. A good spanking was generally considered a legitimate arrow in the parental quiver. We didn't get a lot of them, but the threat was there. Like this: "If I have to stop this car, I don't care who I hit!"

That essential unfairness was key to the deterrent factor. Once the Furies were unleashed it was understood that the consequences were unpredictable. "Straighten up and fly right!" Mom would bark. A classic.

Dad had the advantage of novelty. We didn't see him often enough to get tired of him. "I remember driving home from a conference once," he says. "I'd been away for about a week. There was a romantic song on the radio and I was singing along, and dreaming about Joan and looking forward to being alone. Then I drove up, and a couple of you kids ran out to argue about something, and I could see Joan behind, holding another one, looking very harassed. And my little daydream was over."

Once while attending a lengthy conference in Saskatoon he phoned home to check in. "Are you coming back soon?" Mom asked.

A few days later, he answered. Everything okay? "Well," she said, "I've come down with something, so I have been spending a lot of time lying on the couch. Also, Lynn got hit by a car."

He was on the highway in less than an hour. Lynn wasn't seriously hurt. Dad's conscience was bleeding profusely.

Even when Dad was home he wasn't always present. Dad read a lot and had the reader's ability to focus intently. The kids would wait until he was deep in that faraway zone and take the opportunity to ask for stuff. "Mmm-hmmm," he would murmur, and his assent to a sleepover or camping trip or increase in allowance would immediately be reported to Mom, who as a rule was not fooled.

This little routine almost led to disaster. Eldest brother Joe had begun sleepwalking regularly. One winter night he came padding down the stairs, stark naked, and stood beside Dad's rocking chair. "I'm going out," Joe said.

"Mmm-hmmm," Dad replied.

Joe actually had the front door open and was stepping into a prairie snowstorm by the time Dad emerged from his book fog and grasped the situation.

It may be a little unfair to stand that anecdote up as a metaphor for Dad's general situation, floating somewhere high above the domestic grind. Not too unfair, though. Mom was carrying the load. She was like Hercules, cleaning the Augean stables week after week with little help. But she did not see a hero in the mirror. There always seemed to be a domestic nemesis nearby to torment her. In Regina it was our next-door neighbour, Mrs. Dice. She kept a spotless home with a garden, and always had the wash out early. Mrs. Dice had one son, but Mom didn't really consider that aspect. She saw only her own struggles, felt her own failures. Yet the issues Mom faced were astounding. They ranged from the mundane—illness, injury—to the thoroughly odd. Like head banging.

While still preschoolers, my sister Leslie and I both developed the habit of sitting with our backs to the wall, rhythmically banging our heads. I don't recall how it started, but I do remember it was pleasantly numbing. If no one had ever invented alcohol, a lot of folks would be doing it.

Today there is help and reassurance a click away. The website MamasHealth.com explains: "Kids who are under-stimulated (those who are blind, deaf, bored, or lonely) head bang for stimulation. Children who are over-stimulated (in an overwhelming environment) find the rhythmic movements of head banging soothing. Head banging may be a symptom of autism, Tourette's syndrome, and seizure disorders."

Mom would have loved the Internet in 1962. The bungalow at 5320 Second Avenue may as well have been an island. Alcatraz.

As it turned out neither Leslie nor I suffered from autism, or seizure disorders, or was deaf except when convenient. We were competitive, though. Eventually we both banged holes right through the drywall, each racing to be first to break through. Leslie won, but then I dropped her special Donald Duck bubble bath down one of the holes. Always something.

Kids don't think about a mother's insecurities, and it is a mark of Mom's success that we were so blissfully ignorant. Nor was Mom completely lacking in perspective. She was as fond as anyone of mining good family stories from domestic problems. One epic tale involved my potty training. As I seem to recall from Shakespeare: *Bubble, bubble, toilet trouble.*

The first time they lowered me over that gaping whirlpool whose victims are never again seen, things did not go well. A tender fold of bum skin caught the edge of the booster seat. "It bit me!" I howled. It was every mother's nightmare scenario. I wasn't going near that shark tank ever again.

I was afraid of things that bit. Pine cones. (Yes, they did. On the foot). Toilets, pine cones, and spiders. One of those can still make me soil myself today—if there's a large spider beside the toilet I would rather use Depends.

But as for the specific toilet phobia, mark it down as conquered. I was four years old the day I wandered into the kitchen while Mom was doing dishes. "Well," I said, "guess I'll go potty."

Mom tried to keep her voice casual. "Do you want me to help?"

"Nope," I replied. "But you can come and keep me company if you want."

Perhaps I had been parking logs in my drawers just to get some one-on-one Mom time. Not easy to do with all the little lobbyists running around that house. Competition for an appointment was fierce.

That's why I so cherished that special year when all the kids were in school save me. My turn came eventually though. I would be forced to bid my mother goodbye and make the long, parka-clad waddle down the street and up the lane to Rosemont Elementary.

ROSEMONT WAS actually only a couple blocks from the house. Later in my youth I would tell friends that in Saskatchewan winter attacked with a fury unknown even in neighbouring provinces. The proof? "In Regina the snow went all the way to the top of the school fence."

As an adult I would return to Regina, visit the Rosemont schoolyard, and find that the fence in question had been less than two feet high. It was like a brilliant little mnemonic joke played by the Regina school board. I tip my toque to them.

One of us was less than overjoyed with Regina, and with Rosemont. By 1964 eleven-year-old Joe was already

starting grade eight. A bright student, Joe had been hus-
tled along thanks to the then-in-vogue strategy of allowing sharper students to skip grades. Eventually educators
realized that the social drawbacks outweighed the scholastic advantages.

"I had entered school a year early and then done grades
three and four in the same year," Joe says. "So when I
hit grade five in 1961, I was eight, going on nine. When
I hit grade seven I was tall, a complete beanpole, not well
coordinated, and definitely out of my league in the social
scene. I was being fed all these stories at school about the
grope parties in the park. And being out of the popular
stream, seemingly unaccomplished, I was a target. One
guy who sat behind me stabbed me in the back with his
compass."

Nasty. But nobody was meaner than Noble Galloway.
Galloway was one of Joe's classmates. Even as a kindergarten student I was afraid of Noble Galloway.

One day during sleepy towel time, I committed a crime.
I tugged on another kid's towel while he napped on it,
causing him to bump his head on a table leg. For reasons
I can't recall, he had it coming. My sentence: ten minutes
standing out in the hall. This was a cruel sort of Rus-
sian roulette the teachers played with us—if the principal
walked down the hall during your stretch and found you
standing there you would be hauled down to the office as
an official miscreant, and your parents would be called. If
the principal stayed in his office during your hall sentence
you were safe. What the teachers did not understand was
that the kids in the hall, while afraid of the principal, were
more afraid of Noble Galloway. We were sure if he happened by, he'd kick our asses just to keep limber.

Galloway was a genuine thug. I don't know how many
grades he had failed along the way, but it is safe to say
that by the time he hit grade eight he did not fit into a

little desk with a lot of clearance. Such was his local reign of terror that he once had a mano-a-mano showdown with my own mother.

Mom was looking out the window on Second Avenue and saw a local thug—Galloway, I assumed—dragging a boy down the street. Pausing in front of our house he tied his victim to a telephone pole and set off on some other psychopathic errand. She came out of the house to untie the frightened kid. Moments later Galloway was in her face. Mom stared him down. "I'm going inside to call the police," she said.

Galloway took off.

It's unlikely Galloway made any connection between Joe and Mom. But Galloway didn't need reasons to terrorize boys. Quite the opposite—he and his boys had a brilliantly evil little strategy. Every Monday in the Rosemont schoolyard, Galloway or one of his cronies would announce the name of whichever boy was to be beaten up on the following Friday. The lucky winner would then sweat through the week until X-day, when his ticket would be punched. One week, inevitably, the lottery came up Joe.

Mom wanted to call the school and put a stop to it. Joe begged her not to. "Please, Mom—it will just be worse for me."

Mom did not call. Friday arrived and Joe took his beating.

I remember hearing a story years later to the effect that Galloway had been shot dead during the commission of a crime. It helps me sleep.

BULLYING WAS NOT the issue of greatest concern to my parents. A much bigger threat would have a profound and lasting political effect on the Burgess clan. The catalyst was the Saskatchewan Doctors' Strike of 1962.

In the summer of that year seven-year-old Lynn became seriously ill. How ill? "We were having Jell-O chocolate pudding for dessert," Lynn recalls, "and I didn't want any."

It was a case for the emergency department.

"We sat in the waiting room for hours. I remember looking up at the clock, one of those black-and-white school-type clocks with the big numbers. It was 11:30 p.m. No doctor saw me. At midnight they sent everyone home. The nurse told Dad to bring me back in the morning."

This was not normal procedure at an emergency ward. But these were not normal times for Saskatchewan health care. In 1962 Canadian government—supported health care system did not exist. Tommy Douglas of the CCF (Co-operative Commonwealth Federation) had introduced a plan for universal medical insurance during the 1960 provincial election and won. Douglas then stepped aside to form the New Democratic Party, leaving the Medicare battle to new CCF premier Woodrow Lloyd. After delaying for months Lloyd finally enacted the universal medical insurance legislation scheme on July 1. The same day Saskatchewan doctors went on strike.

Lynn had picked that very week to get sick.

"The next morning I was worse," Lynn says. "I remember Dad trying to dress me as I cried. I kept telling him it hurt when I moved."

"We got to the Grey Nuns Hospital. They pricked my finger to take a blood sample and I responded by throwing up on the floor."

It was explained that Lynn would have to be left at the hospital. However, the strike meant there would be no information available concerning her condition. Our family doctor had offered an opinion before commencing strike action, though: "He thought I had one of two disorders. One was chronic and the other was terminal."

Finding out which would have to wait—for the end of the strike, or of Lynn.

That night in the ward Lynn was feverish. "The girls in my room were running around having a pillow fight. I kept pressing the call button for the nurse, but no one came. Finally in desperation, I got out of bed and went into the hall. All the nurses were huddled around a radio, listening for news of the strike negotiations. I walked toward them and not one of them turned around or noticed me. Just when I got to the nurses' station, I threw up all over the floor. That got their attention."

Ten days later Lynn was not dead. Nor was she much better. They released her anyway. "Mom told me later she was furious. They had to take me back to hospital, this time to the General."

Our doctor was apologetic. But he had not been allowed to communicate with the family during the strike.

The virulent anti-government campaign supported by the *Regina Leader-Post* and the American Medical Association was finally countered by voices from outside the province, including British and European doctors brought in by the Saskatchewan government, who argued that universal medical insurance was not in fact a shortcut to Soviet tyranny. An end to the strike was negotiated after twenty-three days. Medicare had pulled through. So had Lynn.

My parents, however, had caught a new virus from which they would never recover. Previous to that month they had merely leaned toward the New Democrats. Afterward their political convictions would be more pronounced.

Lynn's near-death experience had a silver lining. Like me and my clever pants-soiling routine, she had inadvertently stumbled upon a strategy. "I used to love going to the hospital because Mom would come to visit me, and only me. I felt special. My kidneys were inflamed and the condition was chronic. I was hospitalized three times between the ages of seven and nine. She'd go to the cafeteria and get me a bag of Cheezies or bring me a comic book. What's not to like?

"Mom would probably have had to take the bus to the hospital, would have had to hire a sitter. Dad never came so I expect he was travelling and had the car. I remember how happy I was to see her and how special I felt because I didn't have to share her. After I got out, I added a phrase to my bedtime prayers. I'd pray, 'Please God, let me go to the hospital.'"

When Mom heard Lynn's prayer, she misinterpreted its meaning. "She thought it meant I wasn't happy at home."

TOLSTOY WROTE, "Happy families are all alike." It makes you wonder if he knew any. They're not. They're not even all happy, at least not all the time.

Was 5320 Second Avenue a happy home? Most inmates thought so. Every domestic realm has its particular rhythms. To some extent, ours were a matter of numbers. Five kids and, most days, a single parent meant that a lot of our shaping influences were not top-down, but lateral. In large families, kids tend to raise each other. Older kids take on the roles of middle management—sub-parents delegated to handle cultural and behavioural instruction. Eldest brother Joe ran middle brother Jock with an iron hand and something of a cruel streak. He had the Lucy-and-Charlie Brown habit of staging various athletic contests, which Jock would be allowed to almost win.

Lynn was the real Lucy. Lynn could have eaten Lucy for breakfast. Her primary job was to dominate Leslie, but the task left her plenty of spare time and energy to command the rest of us, a task she performed with the ferocity of Nurse Ratched.

My direct overseer was Jock. Although Joe had been rough on Jock, Jock proved, happily, to be a more benevolent tyrant. We lived a rich and productive fantasy life. At night we swam beneath the covers of our beds, pretending to be sea turtles. By day we recorded rock albums on an old reel-to-reel tape recorder (I played an apple box drum with plastic bowling-pin sticks). All original material. We created a comic book series in which different beings inhabited each of the nine planets (in those innocent days, Pluto still enjoyed planetary status). Neptunians had figure-eight feet and a single eye, set in the middle of a large "X" that crossed their balloon-like heads. They were mean bastards. Mercurians had oval heads and no legs at all—no need, thanks to the jet-propulsion system built right into their floating abdomens. A peaceful race, the Mercurians, unless pushed.

The influence of an older brother, even a benevolent one, can be hard to shake. For years I would not permit myself to form an opinion about a song or a group until I knew what Jock thought. Some years later, at last, came the insurrection. I grabbed a catalogue from the Record Club of Canada—we were members, with absolutely no obligation—and flipped through it randomly. One picture showed a bunch of guys standing in front of some kind of blimp. "I'm ordering that one," I announced. Jock did not approve. Perfect. *Led Zeppelin II* went on to become a favourite of mine for quite a while.

The family always ate dinner together. Discussion was encouraged, if indeed encouragement was needed. Maintaining silence would have required a high-pressure hose. Not that we were constantly engaged in musings about American foreign policy. More often it was about annoying your siblings.

Jock was what they used to call, in those less-clinical days, "fussy." Had our parents been psychiatrists Lynn would have come up with at least three rhyming taunts employing the phrase "obsessive-compulsive." Jock could not eat mashed potatoes with lumps in them; he had something close to a phobia about wet bread. In some school hygiene class he had heard that for optimum digestion one must chew each bite of food thirty-two times. So he did. Lynn would sit beside him and count aloud. "Mom!" Jock would yell. "Make her stop!"

In the end the food was properly chewed and the chewer properly aggravated. It was a true symbiotic relationship.

The rest of the world seemed to think Joan and Bill Burgess were doing a pretty fine job. Both parents were active in the St. John's Sunday school, where their projects included getting the kids to write a Jerusalem newspaper, reporting on the current civil rights movement from a Gospel perspective. As we prepared to leave town in 1965, a St. John's United volunteer named Art Kato wrote a farewell tribute. "When my thoughts come to the Kingdom of God," he wrote, "I often visualize the Burgess family... Early Sunday mornings when their white station wagon drove up [we had traded the Chev for a Ford], full of children, and Bill and Joan carrying armfuls of books and gadgets to work as team teachers, and they would all flock into the side door of our church, it was as if the Kingdom of God was moving in on us."

High praise, that. But for Mom, sometimes it must have felt more like the Apocalypse. She may have been the only one in the neighbourhood likely to accuse Joan Burgess of being a bad mother. Many years later I would get a glimpse of her true emotional state during the Regina days.

In the early 1980s, while I was working as a DJ at a Regina radio station, my parents came from Brandon to visit. Dad and I got excited about visiting the old pink house on Second Avenue. Mom was less enthusiastic. While Dad and I talked our way in for a look around, she waited in the car. We rambled through the place, exclaiming at familiar sights and enjoying ourselves thoroughly.

Later over dinner, Mom confessed: "The sight of that house made me feel physically ill."

There were occasions when even we oblivious kids caught a glimpse of Mom's internal turmoil. Among the most famous: the Pressure Cooker Incident.

It was Mom's birthday. Dad sat by proudly while she unwrapped her annual gift, something Dad and the kids had seen in a shop window looking very pretty—perfect for our mother. Whatever celebration we might have planned would have been sincere and enthusiastic, but five kids under the age of thirteen do not allow for anything truly resembling a day off. So if there was a cake, Mom probably baked it.

Now she received her husband's token of affection: a shiny new pressure cooker. Mom received the gift graciously at first. But contents under pressure can sometimes blow. A few hours later her frustration exploded. "A pressure cooker?" she fumed. "For my birthday? That's the story of my life."

Dad meant well, which probably makes it worse. (To be fair, we helped choose the gift.) And he was heading into a steep learning curve himself. "It was always about her having to play roles she didn't choose," Lynn says. "Minister's wife, homemaker. Dad didn't see—or didn't want to see—how miserable she was."

There were times when her anger broke through.

"When I was about eleven or twelve," Joe says, "I was being a brat about taking out the garbage. She lost it and slapped me across the face.

Years later Mom would tell me that she had done things to me that were not good for me. I was always saying 'Huh? What are you talking about?' But I know incidents like that haunted her."

Busy beetling around at floor level, we rarely noticed the forces working away in the heart and mind of the woman whose attention we competed for. The pain she felt would not truly break loose while we lived in that little pink house on Second Avenue. But the day was coming, nonetheless.

9

CHRISTMAS TOWN

SQUARELY IN the middle of the Canadian map, the province of Manitoba covers an area about the size of Texas. Yet in '65 the population amounted to under a million, roughly half in the capital city of Winnipeg. Demographically, Manitoba looked like a big linoleum floor on which someone had dropped an ice cream cone—one massive lump and some splatters. Brandon was the largest splatter.

Brandon sits in a large valley dug by the Assiniboine River in an otherwise featureless plain, three and a half hours east from Regina, two hours' drive west of Winnipeg. It's a relief, if you actually find it on the way west—fail to turn left on the Trans-Canada, and Brandon is experienced as four gas stations, two motels, a campground, and the gateway to another six hundred miles of flat.

Memories of our family's five years in Regina would take on the quasi-mystical quality that goes with the remembered landscapes of the very young. But Brandon would become my true hometown. The street grid, the little stores and crosstown neighbourhoods, the surrounding fields, would be branded on my brain all the way down to the subconscious. The town still provides the geography of my dreams. Decades and several home bases later, I usually wake up to find that whatever REM scenarios I have just been experiencing were set somewhere on the streets of Brandon.

Our wandering years were over. We had arrived in Christmas Town.

Not that it felt like that to a seven-year-old. Brandon was new territory, with new rules to be learned. The novelty extended even to Christmas itself. Not long after the move, the holiday time-shifted—at least, the part of the holiday that is the entire point of the thing when you're seven.

Christmas morning gift-opening celebrations are a necessity when kids are still loaded with the Christmas 1.0 software, the version where your roof is still a runway and the chimney a legitimate point of entry. At that age Christmas Eve is reserved for lying in bunk beds, vibrating like tuning forks, and discussing doctrinal issues: Can the likes of Prancer and Cupid really match the lightning speed and surprise of Blitzen? Now that we know of the existence of Rudolph, could there be other mutant reindeer we haven't been told about? Why do you even need a Rudolph when you already have a Comet? Is it enough to simply be good, or will Santa grade on the curve? Is it possible to be so good that you get *everything?*

But in our family, that innocent era was over relatively early. A group of five kids generates an efficient grapevine, and the smallest eat from the tree of knowledge prematurely. So my Santa died young. By age five I had already inadvertently ruined a young neighbour's life by blurting out the truth. "But Santa's not real," I told Linda

Yakabovitch helpfully. Her face folded up like a collapsing bag, releasing a bawl of anguish. I'm sorry, Linda. I didn't realize.

By the time we reached Brandon it was clear no more Yuletide subterfuge was needed. And since a United Church minister tends to be rather busy Christmas Day, it was decided with only a modest amount of reluctant whining that from now on the Burgess Christmas would be celebrated on Christmas Eve so Dad could join in.

The new routine hardened quickly, as these things do. Christmas Eve, Dad would take his place in the rocking chair—never a moment too soon—and, surrounded by the impatient, proceed to read out the gift tags one by one. Until one gift was opened and cooed over the next gift would wait. And all on Christmas Eve, no less. We thought ourselves rebels.

Our Christmases were reliably white. So were our Marches, which was less enchanting. Years later, when I was working in a northern Manitoba town, a co-worker and several drunken friends went for a drive into the countryside, none of them wearing proper outerwear. They got a flat tire. My co-worker and all but one of his friends died. In a Manitoba winter, particularly during that pre-cellphone era, car trouble could be fatal.

But summers were shimmering hot and perfumed with the warm scent of prairie grass and railroad tar. There were open fields where you could build forts and smoke stolen cigarettes. Whether it was the size of the town or the innocence of the age, we ran about with a freedom that nowadays might lead to an investigation by Social Services. Kids would play hide-and-seek and kick the can in the early evening—far more dangerous pursuits in those days. Abandoned refrigerators were death traps. There must have been a few small-town hide-and-seek games where quiet little Tommy never did turn up, and the kids just gave up and went home. We never lost anybody as far as I recall, but then we didn't do head counts either.

Mid-sixties Brandon was home to about thirty thousand people. There were two TV channels. People curled. They knew that "cash spiel" could be written as one word or two. Brandon was a farm town, in more ways than one. It served as a retail centre for the surrounding rural community, the place to shop for flour, frozen vegetables, maybe even a new combine. And Brandon schools turned out crops of young hopefuls, destined to spread out around the continent. A medium-sized town with decent schools will always churn out more graduates than it can support. For those with ambition, a Brandon education was like a minor league contract.

And naturally we had the hockey version too. At a big, atmospheric old barn in the middle of town, where you could watch the Brandon Wheat Kings major junior team. Any list of notable Brandon citizens will almost certainly include at least four names—Hall of Famer Turk Broda, Flyers great Ron Hextall, Oilers Stanley Cup—winner Bill Ranford, and Canucks stopper Glen Hanlon. National Hockey League goaltenders have been the city's most prominent export.

That aspect of the local culture did not play to my strengths. I couldn't skate. In Manitoba that was like being Rudolph before the fog rolled in. When they strapped skates on me the blades went sideways and I sort of walked on my ankles. It wasn't pretty. I had to learn to tell jokes.

It wasn't all hockey, thank God. There was a movie theatre. Two, if you counted the drive-in. The selection of films was limited, perhaps, but if you were a kid it guaranteed that you'd occasionally get a chance to see something interesting. When it was someone's birthday you generally went to the movies, and that meant you saw whatever was on. One year on Leslie's birthday it was *The Sand Pebbles*. It ends with Steve McQueen being shot to death by unseen Chinese snipers. Leslie couldn't stop crying.

Another time Mom and Dad took us to the drive-in to see something like *Mary Poppins* or *Chitty Chitty Bang Bang*. But the first half of the double bill turned out to be an arty French vampire flick called *Blood and Roses*, directed by Roger Vadim and starring his post-Brigitte Bardot and pre-Jane Fonda wife, Annette. An obsessed lover believes she is the reincarnation of an ancient vampire, and sees herself covered in blood each time she looks in the mirror. In the end she falls off a cliff and is impaled on a bloody stake. Mom and Dad made us face the back of the car until Julie Andrews or Dick Van Dyke appeared. But we all got glimpses and sort of pieced it together later.

Brandon was no culinary Mecca—it was more of a culinary Kiev. Thanks to the significant local Ukrainian population, church socials and potluck dinners often featured perogies, cabbage rolls, and borscht. Yet somehow you could never find that great cuisine in a restaurant. British immigrants still dominated, and that sealed our fate as far as restaurant fare went. Or perhaps it is just the cuisine of small towns, then and now—chicken or egg salad, Denver sandwiches, fries, and hamburgers that no travel guide would ever describe as "undiscovered treasures." At Brandon diners the myth of small-town quality ran up against fly-specked reality. Ethnic food? Soo's Chop Suey House. Later on, the exciting seventies would bring in a few pizza joints. Two of them were chains, but one had real Italians.

Downtown was still the place to shop at street corner department stores like the Metropolitan, Kresge's, and especially Eaton's. It was the golden age for a lot of waddling retail dodos, blissfully unaware that someday the predators would come.

A few of my school friends and I would spent our after-school time downtown shoplifting useless items for the sake of theft. I once stole a plastic Santa in July. As we wandered the aisles of the Met, floorwalkers would trail us doggedly. Considering the ultimate fate of the Met and the entire downtown retail environment, those grim-faced employees probably should have been out hunting Sam Walton.

The Wheat City had one institution that set it apart from the average prairie town. Brandon University was smaller than Winnipeg's two post-secondary institutions, albeit with a music department that punched above its weight. Later alumni include violin prodigy James Ehnes. But the school's most famous alumnus graduated in 1930, back when it was known as Brandon College. Socialist icon Tommy Douglas, named the greatest Canadian of all time in a 2004 CBC national poll, left Brandon College with a master's degree in sociology. It is said that Douglas and Stanley Knowles, another future giant of Canadian socialist politics, had a particular technique for redistributing wealth. Douglas would offer to bet anyone that Knowles could read through a student essay twice and recite it by heart. The young and relatively well-heeled would then learn to their cost that Knowles possessed a photographic memory.

Douglas absorbed liberal theology from Brandon College professors who inveighed against fundamentalism and promoted the gospel of social justice. Forty years later Bill Burgess set up shop across the street at Knox United, ready to take up the same banner.

Since its founding in 1925, the United Church of Canada had been a home for social activists. But as Canada's largest Protestant denomination it naturally came to include believers of almost every theological stripe. The Knox congregation was thus an uneasy mix of liberal and conservative traditions, and in that regard it was Brandon writ small.

The presence of the university ensured that Brandon would have its coterie of liberals. But we were not quite Austin, Texas, a leftist fortress surrounded by ideological hostiles. Brandon was a solid bastion for the federal Progressive Conservative Party. The personification of that political dominance was Walter Dinsdale, the local PC Member of Parliament. Dinsdale was not a flashy sort, but those who challenged him would discover that he hadn't gotten a vice grip on the riding by accident.

At the provincial level the little city's split personality started to show—the east side of town elected a New Democratic Party member just as regularly as the Westsiders went Tory.

We Burgesses were Westsiders. But not legitimately. Dad's job paid ten thousand a year. Our first five years in town we lived in the church-owned manse on a street called Cedar Bay. Doctors lived on either side. There was a swimming pool next door. In terms of relative income our family might just as well have pulled up in a big trailer and plugged into the neighbour's utilities with a hose and a long extension cord.

We all had well-off playmates. Once I slept over at a buddy's place, and in the morning his mom served waffles with strawberries and aerosol whipped cream. It was like science fiction. The owner of Brandon's only local TV station lived around the bay—his kids had G.I. Joes and all the top-of-the-line toys, and there was a Buick Wildcat parked in the garage. Their mom didn't really look like a mom.

Lynn recalls visiting the home of her friend down the street. "She had a pool table in her beautifully finished basement. Their house didn't just have an upstairs and a downstairs—it had 'levels.' They had wall-to-wall carpeting, back when that was something you wanted. She never had to worry either about whether she had enough outfits to make it through the week without repeating."

And there was the neighbour's swimming pool. My sisters spied on it, rapt as two supermodels outside a bakery. Had our backstroking neighbours ever lifted their gaze beyond the fence and toward the upper windows of our house they would have screamed in terror. Glowing faintly in the dark were the unblinking orbs of green-eyed monsters. "I still remember Leslie and I standing on her bed by the window," Lynn says, "looking out at the pool, and hearing that sound of the diving board as one of them dove in."

Looking to the sky, a bathing suit clutched tightly in her fist, Lynn made a solemn vow. "As God is my witness," she cried. "I'll never be pool-less again."

Or so I assume. But while Lynn had to play Scarlett O'Hara, I was free to be Huck Finn. Envy is not such a big issue for eight-year-old boys. G.I. Joes and strawberry waffles notwithstanding, I had as many marbles as the next kid. And as far as pools were concerned, Jock and I were men of action. One day we dug a massive hole in the backyard and filled it with water. It lacked certain amenities, such as filtration and visibility. But it had something better—frogs. We caught over a dozen in a nearby ravine and brought them to their new home, a paradise of amphibian community planning. Like so many socially engineered utopias, it would all go horribly wrong. Even before Mom demanded that we replace every shovelful of dirt, our tenants had vacated. We learned this one Sunday on the way home from church. Approaching our street we saw at least a dozen flat, spotted discs of frog leather, scattered over the road. Where they were headed we would never know. At any rate, none of the neighbours had stopped for them. We all crossed the road more carefully after that.

Frogs are not enough for everyone. As the eldest two, Joe and Lynn had a keen sense of our relative economic position. Plus, Lynn and Les were girls, with all that that entailed. Lynn in particular felt that lack of status: "I remember Mom trying to explain to me why we didn't have money for something I wanted, trying to explain that we were struggling a bit financially. I screamed at her: 'Don't tell me about that stuff! I don't want to know about that!'"

We were not poor. In fact Mom and Dad had managed to scrape together five thousand dollars in savings to buy a cottage at Clear Lake, seventy miles north of Brandon, a summer spot destined to become hallowed ground for the Burgess clan. But on a day-to-day basis we operated very close to the bone. In a professional neighbourhood our home was a lower-middle-class quarantine. Hamburger seemed like a luxury. We ate a lot of Puffed Wheat. Mom mixed powdered milk with the real stuff. Any fresh fruit was carefully rationed. I got a lot of hand-me-downs, and Mom cut all our hair.

Living on a street full of doctors had some benefits, at least on those occasions when we kids tried to kill ourselves. No one tried harder than me.

The accident that came closest to killing me was Jock's fault, mostly. One night at dinner he suggested I was clumsy. It was a vile slander that had to be answered. After dinner I walked across the street to the big construction site at Vincent Massey School.

They were building a new wing with a big gymnasium and more classrooms. The site was not fenced off. Before the modern culture of litigation took hold, construction sites were playgrounds for young boys—obstacle courses, full-size Stalingrad sets for urban war games. I wandered in and started exploring.

In one roofless room a diagonal row of reinforcing rods climbed the wall, like a tree-house staircase. Clumsy, am I? I scrambled up to the top of the wall and began to walk along its narrow length. Below me, double rows of rebar stuck up from the unfinished floor like bamboo stakes in a booby-trapped pit. At the intersection of two walls a large wooden board was propped up. I steadied myself on the board and reached my foot into space, intending to step on another metal bar. The board I leaned on had not been nailed down, and toppled over. I wavered, wobbled, and pitched forward into space.

It seemed to me that I was going down head-first. In fact it was my feet that touched concrete first, my knees a millisecond later. A week or so later I would notice that my bruised and bloodied knees hurt like hell. But it would take that long for those particular nerves to be heard above the sensory din. I had bigger problems higher up. A piece of rebar had struck me just below my mouth, splitting my lip and thrusting deep into my cheek. Doctors would later say that the placement was almost surgical—an inch higher would have cost me an eye or pierced my brain; an inch or two lower would have severed my jugular vein. As it was, I was merely bleeding like the runner-up in a sabre duel.

My hand jerked to my mouth. It came back dripping. I screamed, and it seemed to me that the noise of all the nearby Little League games suddenly ceased. I lurched up and out of the room. There was an obstacle in front of me—a little wooden divider, no more than a foot and a half high. I slumped down in front of it, momentarily defeated. Later it would be explained to me that this temporary helplessness was probably the result of shock. I sat staring at that little wall for what seemed quite a while, steadily losing more blood, before I could summon the appropriate urgency. Then I was up again, over the obstacle, through the maze of unfinished rooms, and out to the street. My path must have been marked by a dribbling red trail, like little Jeffy in a slasher-movie version of *The Family Circus*.

We had, as I mentioned, doctors on both sides. Our doctor neighbour to the north was not a family pal. His wife had threatened legal action if Burgess kids kept throwing crabapple cores into their yard. On this evening he was out mowing the lawn and saw me staggering across the road, holding my face. He raced out to meet me, pried my hands away, and quickly surveyed the damage. As he bundled me toward our front door, he called out to my parents to start the car. "I knew something was wrong," Jock said later, "when I came home and noticed that the green facecloth in the bathroom was now red."

Dad ran red lights as we raced to the hospital. I recall touching my face and wondering what that unfamiliar mass of chaotic flesh could possibly look like. In the operating room they pulled a sheet over me as though I were a cadaver—it contained one cut-out square, positioned over the wound. Later Mom said her clearest memory was of the surgeons talking to me beforehand: "We can give you the kind of anesthetic that will knock you out, Steve—but it would be better for us if we don't."

Go with the local, I said. Mom says she choked up a bit about that.

They stitched me up, but more trouble was coming. The metal bar that impaled my face had been rusty and generally unfit for human consumption. Soon I was running a fever. My cheek swelled up like a helium balloon, my teeth pulled shut, my skin became so tight and shiny you could actually see your reflection. Naturally Lynn would stop by the couch and use my cheek to apply her lipstick. Jock told me jokes to hear me try to laugh without being able to open my mouth. I lived on A&W milkshakes, which was great, except the straws were too fat to fit through my clenched teeth.

We didn't sue. Mom didn't believe in that approach. But she had a few words with an embarrassed school board. Fences and locked gates soon closed up the construction site.

I was out of school for weeks. The day I returned an excited classmate ran up. "Where'd they shoot ya?"

My other near-death experience was considerably more amusing. It happened after a family trip to Dairy Queen. Each kid would get to choose one item, and dad would buy a bag of Dilly Bars for the freezer. My habitual choice was a miraculous bit of ice-cream engineering called a Jet or, as we called it, a push-up. It was a little cardboard tube of ice cream equipped with a stick that pushed up the bottom as you went along. For my money, it provided a more interactive experience than a simple cone.

The drive itself was a big part of it all. We'd load up with ice cream and just cruise around town—three in the front, four in the back. Even if seat belts had been standard equipment back then there wouldn't have been nearly enough of them. On long highway drives in those old station wagons we were completely untethered, bouncing around like golf balls in a dryer.

On this excursion I was wedged in at the end of the back seat row, working that Jet. Dad had driven out near the edge of town, where cars start to speed up on their way out to Highway 1. As he turned left off 1A, the side door swung open. I was pitched out, skidding down the asphalt on my face. I am told that there was a vehicle coming toward me at considerable speed. I never saw it.

As soon as I stopped skidding I was on my feet, running toward the ditch. It wasn't a matter of self-preservation— I was chasing my Jet. It had rolled into the gravel, taking a considerable portion of chocolaty goodness with it, and my eyes were on the prize. The vehicle passed safely behind as I snatched the Jet out of the dirt. Then the road rash kicked in and I started to cry.

If a frozen treat saved my life, it's not so surprising. Those Dairy Queen trips were big events. Discretionary spending was tight and allowances miniscule. A push-up or a dipped cone was a solid recreational benefit. What passed for luxury in our house would never be recognized as such elsewhere on our street.

Our parents were concerned that we not feel self-conscious about our relatively low financial status. And while we may not have kept up with the Joneses, we didn't stand out for the wrong reasons either. We weren't short of Christmas gifts. When I prayed fervently for Hot Wheels to whatever deity ruled Christmas—a kid's theology can be fuzzy on that point—Mom and Dad were there on Christmas Eve to say, "Amen."

Besides, when it comes to finances, what matters, psychologically, is progress. An increase of allowance from ten cents to fifteen means big forward momentum. Slipping backward is the hard part. In fact, it turns out our little church ghetto might have put us in the perfect situation. A 2008 study out of Germany looked at economic satisfaction in small neighbourhoods and concluded: "Not only do individuals feel better off as their own income grows, they also feel better as they live with richer neighbours."

So maybe we were getting a little splash from that swimming pool after all. And things were indeed on the upswing. Mom had started working.

10

SPOON UND DRANG

MOM NEVER smoked. And she was certainly not the impressionable sort. So I never heard her express any opinion about Virginia Slims cigarettes or their insidiously brilliant advertising campaign. Philip Morris launched the brand in 1968 as a longer, slimmer cigarette that would presumably look a little more elegant than whatever Frank Sinatra had hanging off his lip. Ostensibly the Virginia Slims advertising slogan referenced the fact that it used to be illegal for women to smoke in public. But if ad men used the word "zeitgeist" in '68, then somebody must have dropped it in the boardroom when they unveiled the catchphrase: "You've come a long way, baby." The evil bastards were onto something.

Those ads featured gowned and bejewelled models with knowing smiles and no evidence of any childbearing history. Yet strict truth-in-advertising regulations would have required Philip Morris to put my mother in those pictures. If you wanted to see the rising curve of female empowerment in the 1960s, you couldn't do better than to hitch a ride with Joan Burgess. She was on the move.

In 1964 Mom had been in full domestic lockdown, herding five pre-pubescent kids with little assistance. By 1974 Mom had completed her degree and was well into a teaching career, one that had already steered her family through a serious professional and financial crisis. An impressive but far from painless progression.

There are moments in the history of nations and of people when everything changes—attacks and disasters, usually. But even in the absence of some specific tragedy, there is a tendency to look for a turning point. Choosing one catalytic moment in a life is not always realistic. For the sake of a more dramatic narrative long months and years of incremental change are reduced to an incident.

Yet it always seemed to me that there had been just such a moment in our home. It was the Wooden Spoon Incident. This was the only time I can remember when we kids got a taste of how some others live, a brief visit to the nightmare world where children are hardened by fear and perpetual wariness.

It happened at Cedar Bay. By this time Mom had already taken her first job—secretary at Great-West Life Insurance, at a salary of fifty-five dollars a week. The job was more a matter of pressing financial need than a step on the road to female emancipation. But it did inadvertently prove to Mom that crisis and drama were not confined solely to the domestic realm. One day her boss did not show up for work. Customers were calling to complain about lapsed policies. Forced to search his desk for the appropriate files, Mom found piles of undeposited cheques—thousands of dollars worth of policy holder payments, simply stuck into a drawer by a man who was either experiencing a mental breakdown or had misunderstood a fundamental principle of banking.

Mom helped clean up after that mess. But she had her own storms brewing.

Family memories are almost always Rashomon stories. Everyone remembers things a little differently. Dad now recalls the Wooden Spoon Incident as basically his fault, the aftermath of some marital argument that spilled over to affect the children. But from the kids' point of view it's always about the kids. In this case, Lynn.

In 1966 Lynn was a hellcat—twelve years old, stubborn, openly defiant, possessed of a wide streak of Grandma. She would have been the equivalent of an attic full of squirrels even as an only child, never mind one of a quintet. Lynn sassed back and refused direct orders. And yet the trigger this time was trivial, the proverbial last straw. "I had left my school books on the stairs going up," Lynn says. "Mom screamed at me to take my books upstairs like I was supposed to. I recall—although who knows what's accurate anymore—that she threw the books at me. Not in a way that would cause injury, just to make the point. I must have yelled back or something."

Mom went into the kitchen, grabbed a wooden spoon, and headed upstairs. Lynn sat sulking in her bedroom—at this point, a familiar drill. But Lynn's usual bravado evaporated suddenly. She found herself face to face with a level of rage that was new and terrifying. Mom was sparking and crackling like a toaster in a bathtub. She turned Lynn over her knee and brought the spoon down again and again.

Then the situation escalated. With Lynn howling upstairs and the kids scrambling for hiding places, Dad interceded. To the astonishment of all he took the spoon away from Mom and swung it against her backside. "See how you like it," he said.

I retreated to the basement and tried to stuff myself under the couch. Upstairs the gods waged war. Dad was our champion. I was afraid of my mother. Many times in the past I knew I'd stepped over the line and was facing justice, and there must also have been times when I sensed it was just a good day to stay out of the way. This was a different feeling. Mom was transformed. She made it partway down the stairs before Dad coaxed her back. "You think this is over," she said, shaking a finger at us. "It isn't."

But it was. She drove away and left us in the house, not returning until the kids were in bed hours later.

The Wooden Spoon Incident had been an explosion of anger from a woman proud of her self-discipline. "She was out of control," Lynn says. "And she wasn't known to be out of control."

We could be unruly kids, certainly. But until that episode we had not really grasped that we were playing with matches at a gas station.

Mom did, though. The combustible elements had been there for years. Here was a woman of keen intelligence who had met her future husband at Queen's University, a woman whose curiosity and desire for intellectual and spiritual connection had been largely sidelined by her primary role as manager of a human puppy mill. With a manipulative, critical, emotionally domineering mother still looming over her world and a well-meaning husband who simply wasn't grasping the situation, Joan Burgess struggled with anger, guilt, and a powerful sense of her own inadequacy, exacerbated by the experience of raising five young children. The fact that the other domestic wizards she watched with envy were dealing with a fraction of her workload did not seem to penetrate. She believed she was failing as a mother.

"Those were our roughest days," Dad said later.

The rest of us rarely understood what forces were roiling inside our mother's psyche. Which is the way

Mom wanted it. No one else was to be made to suffer for problems that she considered her own. As usual, Mom's course of action would be the one her own mother would never have chosen—ruthless self-examination. Mom made the decision to see a psychiatrist.

Brandon Mental Health Centre opened in 1891 as the Asylum for the Insane. A campus of red brick dorms, its location on the northern shoulder of the river valley made it the embodiment of that schoolyard term "the house on the hill" (whereas the "funny farm"—an agricultural research facility called the Brandon Experimental Farm—was located just down the slope). The Brandon Mental, as we called it, perched above the city like the home of Norman Bates. Psychiatric analysis may never be an experience that people list on resumés, but in the mid-sixties the stigma was particularly powerful. It must have taken courage to climb that hill. When Dad suggested to our neighbour (the doctor with the swimming pool) that he was thinking of following Mom's lead and going for some psychiatric counselling himself, the doctor was against it. "He didn't want word getting out that the minister at his church was seeing a psychiatrist," Dad recalls. "I remember driving up there and hoping no one would see me."

Mom had demons. But, Lynn believes, "It was Dad who had to change the most."

The direct results of Mom's psychiatric visits were not particularly helpful. Over the years Mom would have criminally bad luck with doctors. As she described it later, her psychiatrist refused to look her in the eye during their sessions, which concluded with the doc tossing out a prescription for pills that she never took. "After a couple of visits," Mom said, "I felt like I should keep going back for his sake. I felt bad for him."

Brandon being a fairly small place, I would later become good friends with several of that psychiatrist's sons. One of the older brothers was my classmate in grade ten. I was fifteen; he was twenty-two. A study of that family's home life could have been some sociologist's ticket to lasting fame. The clan matriarch, an erratic Englishwoman who spoke fondly of hanging out with Joe Cocker back in the Old Country, would sit in the living room with a glass of hard liquor and the TV turned up full blast to drown out the family rock band practising at concert volume in the basement. Dr. Dad sat in the kitchen with his head in the newspaper, while family members screamed at each other, not necessarily because they were fighting, but just to be heard over the tarmac-level noise. Pot and cigarette smoke swirled overhead, and mixed drinks were a recurring design motif. They owned a large dog that habitually knocked over lamps. An hour spent in that house seemed like some kind of astronaut stress test. A favourite family anecdote I heard involved one of the brothers who, as a tyke, stole Mom's bag of pot and sold it on the street—but only charged a dollar. Kids!

And supporting the family was Dr. V., the psychiatrist. Clearly he didn't bring his work home with him. (Yet it must also be said that this family, as far as I could see, was close, mutually supportive, and happier than most. Once again, Tolstoy's theory of happy families blows.)

In spite of our neighbour's concerns, my father decided to suck it up, climb that spooky hill up to Norman Bates's house, and go see a shrink. "I was so embarrassed walking up those steps."

Dad's concerns quickly vanished. He and the psychiatrist, a Dr. B., established a great rapport. Eventually Dad would return for several sessions. What exactly they discussed is lost now, but it seems the doc was among those bold pioneers out there on the frontiers of the mid-sixties mind. "Dr. B. was a wonderful guy. At our last session he gave me a book—sort of a gentle way to say that our time together was over."

The book was *Psychedelic Prayers and Other Meditations,* by Timothy Leary.

Only a few years later Dr. B. would be found dead in his basement, where he had set up a private rifle range. It was a self-inflicted gunshot wound. Of course there was always the chance that it had been an accident.

Both my parents continued on the paths of self-examination via the available means of the era. That meant a lot of encounter groups. Like brown-and-orange colour schemes and harvest-gold bathroom appliances, encounter groups are now indelibly linked with the seventies. But it was during the sixties that they really started to proliferate. Encounter groups were a kind of non-traditional psychotherapy in which people discussed their feelings and uncovered deep-seated emotions. They could prove useful. They could also turn into a nasty kind of amateur hour. Generally encounter groups were run not by psychologists but by laypeople. Later permutations included all-nude groups, twenty-four-hour marathon sessions, and a particularly ugly variant in which one participant was singled out and attacked. Even in the gentler sessions participants would engage in hard questioning of other attendees' responses or perceived evasions—situations that held the potential for some vicious bullying.

One day in 1968 Dad was participating in a group being run by a personal friend. It would still prove traumatic.

The night before, Dad reported to the group, he'd had a disturbing dream. He was enraged, chasing someone who'd done him wrong. There was murder in his heart. The man he pursued was some sort of authority figure. "Who?" the group leader asked.

"I don't know," Dad answered. "I can't see."

The moderator badgered. "Who is it? Come on, Bill."

"It's my father," he said finally.

It was a shock to say it. His father had been a kind and good man. But little Billy had lost his mother at age seven—taken away in an ambulance, never to be seen again, alive or dead, no chance for a seven-year-old boy to say goodbye. Someone has to be held responsible for that. Now Dad found himself crying uncontrollably. An emotional gusher had been tapped.

The ultimate goal of any therapeutic program is for patients to heal themselves. Mom would never be one to live the unexamined life. Her desire for self-knowledge would lead her to seek counsel and companionship from like-minded souls all her life. It would also lead her to a new career. Which is what really changed everything.

ONE SUNDAY morning not long after we arrived in town, Dad preached a sermon that happened to work in a reference to a magazine story he'd seen. A parishioner paused on the way out to shake his hand. "Never heard a Knox minister talk about *Redbook* before," he cracked.

His name was Keith Cooper. He was the superintendent of Rolling River School Division, covering a district just north of Brandon with a progressive approach that belied its rural location. The Coopers would become lifelong family friends. It would be Keith who opened the door to Mom's new career.

Keith was looking for a guidance counsellor for a small-town high school. Someone who would not frighten the rural superintendents—no sensitive college longhairs, freshly graduated and eager to shape young minds via the latest innovative strategies. The better Keith got to know Joan Burgess, the more convinced he was that she would be a perfect candidate. A quiet, forty-ish mother of five would not frighten any of the appointed burghers whose approval was required. More crucially it seemed to Keith that Joan was made for the job—empathetic, a listener rather than a talker, possessed of insight, compassion, and plenty of first-hand experience with kids. She was also a veteran of human relations and leadership seminars—my parents were big on those, going back to their days teaching Sunday School together in Regina.

And perhaps best of all, Joan Burgess had a low threshold for nonsense.

Once at Knox, Dad and his assistant came up with what they thought was a brilliant idea—a "wrong way" seminar. When participants (including Mom) arrived, the room was a mess. The stated goal was impossibly vague, the language impenetrable, the leaders' behaviour arrogant. Their clever plan was to do everything wrong and then evaluate the results. Most of the participants were confused, but Mom was enraged. "When we got home there was an explosion," Dad says. "She thought it had been a betrayal, a denial of everything we stood for—dishonest, manipulative, and cruel."

Compassionate, yet intolerant of bullshit—perfect qualities for dealing with high school students. Keith Cooper told Joan that if she were to return to school for another year to get her teaching certificate, he could guarantee her a job when she graduated.

So it would turn out. Our mom became a student at Brandon University. She graduated with her teaching certificate in 1968. In the fall of 1969 Joan Burgess began commuting twenty-six miles every day to Rivers, a farming town of fewer than two thousand inhabitants, where she was the guidance counsellor at the grandly named Rivers Collegiate Institute. Later she would begin teaching English classes. She was good at it.

Mom's new career had some practical implications at home. Two incomes meant the arrival of stuff. A microwave oven, for instance—a major signpost of early-seventies prosperity. It was now possible for us to melt cheese over a piece of bread even while that bread sat on a plain, miraculously unsinged paper plate. Men landing on the moon was impressive too, but it didn't have the same immediate impact.

A little something else came our way around that time—a home. A real house, owned and operated by the Burgess family, located at 54 Clement Drive. It was a relatively new ranch-style place with a deceptively large amount of floor space and a big finished basement. There was a crabapple tree in the backyard, and the apples weren't even sour. We all took to the house immediately. It had some very cool oddities, like a shower room in the basement. Only one nozzle, but in a full-size room with a tile floor. Very decadent. In later years it would prove particularly useful when someone—say Leslie's friend Cindy—would drink too much and throw up on herself. You could just drag her into the shower room and turn on the taps.

No one loved the house more than Mom, for whom 54 Clement meant a kind of freedom many women would never understand. Living in church housing had been perfectly okay for the kids. It was a constant nettle to Mom. Her simplest domestic decisions could always be overruled by that board of penny-pinching tyrants, the manse committee. Now all that was over. Death to tyrants, hello interior design.

A new home with a microwave and a ridiculously huge shower and rooms and rooms of freedom—the benefits of our new double-income reality were there to be enjoyed. And there was another, less tangible effect. It was the slow, cumulative influence of example. Mom and Dad both had real careers and clearly made family decisions together. There were no vetoes. As the seventies progressed, the ideals of feminism were being asserted with increasing force in public debate. But there was no debate at 54 Clement. Equality of the sexes was second nature at our place. We experienced it every day.

Meanwhile Dad's career at Knox United made him a natural community leader. In the early seventies he was given an honourary appointment to the Brandon University board of governors. Other local luminaries on the board included MP Walter Dinsdale. The appointment was a sign of respect. It would also demonstrate the dark adage that no good deed goes unpunished.

One day in early 1972 there was a Board of Governors meeting. The regular chairman being absent, Dad took the chair. Among the issues voted upon was the installation of condom vending machines on the university campus. The vote was 7–2 in favour. Dinsdale voted no, and he was not prepared to let it go.

Walter Dinsdale was first elected to Parliament in 1951. He would remain cemented to the Brandon–Souris seat until his death thirty-one years later. Dinsdale's name rarely appeared in Hansard, the Parliamentary record—for that, it's necessary to stand up and speak. But he knew his constituents. He knew that beyond the boardroom of Brandon University folks weren't likely to be quite so progressively inclined as the good governors.

So, shortly after the vote Dinsdale recruited a teenager to go buy a condom from the new machine. Success. Condom in hand, the MP then alerted the media. A popular Winnipeg radio talk show host was soon trumpeting the news that Brandon University had begun teaching its host community how sexual morality is for suckers. Worst of all, it was said, this corruption of local youth had begun with a Board of Governors vote chaired by one William Burgess—a local United Church minister.

The Knox congregation split. Pro- and anti-Burgess camps neatly described the odd nature of both Brandon and the local United Church community, a mixture that ranged from retired farm folk to young academics. It threatened to become a battle for the soul of the congregation itself, with Dad's supporters eager for him to stick it out and battle the reactionaries.

The local paper filled with angry letters. Our phone would ring late at night. I remember one call—a man asked for my dad, who was out. The caller then requested I inform Dad that he was a dirty old man, and hung up. I passed it along.

One evening Dad was meeting with two other local United Church ministers to plan an upcoming Easter service. Instead he broke down and wept. "What the hell," one of the ministers said. "We've got an organist who's always asking to play Bach. She'll be happy to get the chance."

The planning meeting gave way to a therapy session, as Dad unloaded his grief about what was coming. He often said that he was never more grateful for an act of friendship.

Dad had no stomach to tear his church apart. To considerable disappointment and some bitterness from his would-be ideological militia, he resigned from Knox United. A career that had begun with a doctorate in ministry and subsequently carried our family across four provinces and the state of Ohio was finished.

Dad would be unemployed for months. His next job would be in the Department of Agriculture. It was a twist of fate that made Mom's career more important than ever.

Nineteen seventy-two was not exactly a spice garden for the family. No doubt we spent our days preoccupied with the issues and dramas of the day. But a moment of reflection taken that year would have paid dividends. Mom had turned the corner. She had a career, and our family had a new dynamic. For his part Dad, a man born in 1925 and married in 1950, had awakened to the changing nature of his marriage and his world. His perspective had been widened—with a crowbar, more or less, but it did happen. Their relationship had undergone the sort of transformation frequently associated with divorce. Faced with the level of unhappiness and dissatisfaction Mom had been experiencing, most people would throw it all away and start fresh. Many years later she told me that either because of the times, the circumstances, or the individuals, divorce just wasn't an option. "With five kids," she said, "it was just something we wouldn't consider. You just didn't do it."

11

WHO KILLED MOM?

A LMOST EIGHTY-THREE years old but unlikely to get there, Mom lies on her death bed, inert save for that terrible, hard breathing She's been back and forth to the hospital like a city bus, but now comes the terminus. Mom is dying. Perhaps it is time to start the blame game. Surely someone must be responsible.

Recently a friend of mine talked about her father's death. "It helps to have somewhere to focus your anger," she said.

And where is hers targeted, I asked?

"On Dad's wife," my friend says firmly. "She didn't want him to go on living."

Pretty harsh. And how old was Dad? "Ninety-five," she said. "But his own dad lived to be ninety-seven!"

There's not much you can say about natural causes. That's why few celebrities ever die of them. Not many famous cases end with the official coroner's report. Several historians claim Napoleon was poisoned. Princess

Diana was murdered, according to Mohamed Al-Fayed. Nirvana lead singer Kurt Cobain, a notorious depressive and veteran of suicide attempts, was found with a shotgun and a suicide note. His widow hired a private investigator. The detective's verdict: murder. Marilyn Monroe was purportedly killed by the Kennedys, who were in turn killed by the CIA, and the Mafia, and Fidel Castro. Michael Jackson could not be allowed to live—he knew too much. And do we really know who shot Bambi's mom?

Generally speaking important people do not simply expire. So it seems only right to afford the same status to my mother. She's important too. Someone must be killing her. There are solid suspects.

Grandma's role in the crime has been examined. Medical malpractice has played its part. But there are others in the perp lineup. Surely her husband took years off her life—that can't be helped. Then there are the children. None had motive, but all had opportunity—and time to make it look like natural causes. Damning evidence is easy to find.

The mere fact of our arrival in a six-year span would have been enough to kill some women, never mind raising, corralling, chasing, and trying to keep us above ground despite a veritable medical catalogue of illnesses and a litany of accidents showing astonishing creativity. On the disease front I ran the usual gamut of measles, mumps, chicken pox, and bronchitis, but also went the extra mile by picking up scarlet fever. Who knows how many days the stress subtracted from Mom's lifespan?

Joe spent some time in a cult. Lynn was a hellcat capable of such venom that Mom wept and truly came to believe her daughter despised her. Jock frequently made our house the centre of a social circle that, while sparkling, could have resulted in charges of aiding and abetting the corruption of minors; Leslie added more of the same.

Yet these are mild diversions, a lifeless pile of pale-pink herrings. You want the real suspect, the one who stands, hands dripping red, at the end of a long litter trail of circumstantial evidence. Who do you like for this murder? I'm your man.

I don't know if I really shortened poor Mom's life. The fact is that she surely lived a lot longer than most medical people expected. Perhaps she was really too tough to be killed off by the likes of us. But I think it's fair to say I contributed more stress to her life than any immediate relative except her own mother.

The sordid chronicle of my adolescence will make it clear what my mother was forced to deal with. But first, a small sample—the story of an early-morning bicycle ride.

I was probably about eighteen years old, still living in the basement, the only child left at home. I had been at an all-night party, and as morning dawned I stumbled out to my bike to ride home. I remember only little snapshots from that ride, but they are enough to confirm that I made the entire crosstown ride while looking straight down at the ground. Stop signs ambled through the corner of my eye as I trundled on blindly, spared from death or injury by dumb luck and the fact that I lived in a town small enough for the streets to be deserted very early on a Sunday morning.

A witness supplied the end of the story; I wasn't really there. The sun was already up and kids were playing on the street when my mother saw me pedal into the driveway and stop. Not stop and dismount, but simply stop pedalling, pausing upright for a wondrous moment before toppling over, bike and all, like a tipped cow. With a crowd of kids pointing and laughing, Mom had to walk out to the driveway and drag me into the house. In fitting punctuation to a perfect experience of pain for her and humiliation for me, I had pissed myself.

This was just a random morning. Not the beginning of the problem, nor the end; not a trivial incident, but not the worst either. Only a snapshot of the sadness, stress, and anxiety I inflicted on my mother, a woman with four other kids and a full-time job. Maybe it wasn't murder, exactly. But what I put her through was certainly criminal.

I WAS A GOOD kid once. People liked me. I was cute. My brothers and sisters called me Chicken Hawk, after the determined little character from Bugs Bunny cartoons, because of my adorably pudgy little cheeks.

My eleventh birthday was less than two weeks after Woodstock. It was an exciting time, unless you were eleven and living in Brandon. The local radio station played Perry Como and Al Martino and Bobby Sherman. I had no idea who James Brown was. All that counter-culture excitement seemed to be happening on a distant world to lucky, older people. People who took drugs.

Some kids find purpose and constructive fun in athletics and clubs. It's not as though I didn't try. I just sucked at it. For me, the only truth to be found in physical activity was this: young males achieve social dominance through mastery of the very skills I lacked. Jock used to reminisce about witnessing the highlight of my Little League career—a very loud foul ball. As for manly prowess, I was the only kid in my Cub Scout troop with a naked sleeve, empty of stars and merit badges. It is my contention that this reflected a subtle rejection of authority rather than simple ineptitude. Although I had ineptitude as well. One year my wood shop teacher presented me with a plaque adorned with a question mark and the inscription, "Royal Order of Wood Butchers." True story.

Neither athlete nor craftsman, I was nevertheless a precocious lad. Pretentious, even, if that taunt can be thrown at anyone so callow. (At age thirteen I declared myself to be a Communist—probably the best time of life to flirt with Communism). I was determined to demonstrate an ability to keep up with my elders. Sharing the house with older brothers and sisters who were already getting into high school–level misbehaviour, I wanted in. In particular I longed to join in with Jock and his friends.

Three years older, Jock was part of a remarkable circle. They were, in my eyes, a young Renaissance group. Even now those teenagers live on in my memory as paragons of vibrant creativity and preternatural sophistication, permanently enshrined as an ideal I will never match. Our basement was the centre of their social activity. They drank but were not drunkards by Manitoba standards, and their gatherings seemed to me more like salons than teenage booze-ups. Once they organized a square dance— pushed the furniture to one side and swung around to bluegrass music. We had an old, out-of-tune piano down there that nobody in our family could play, but Jock's friend Fat (he wasn't) was a music student. One late night Dad came storming down the stairs to break up a noisy party and ended up sitting on the stairs tapping his feet while Fat banged out melodies.

There were plenty of influences to corrupt a young mind in those days. Drugs were an integral part of the scene for a questing young person of the early seventies. Being a worldly youngster involved delving into the books of Carlos Castaneda, who told of other dimensions accessible through powerful Mexican substances. Happily, this drug mystique did not extend to anything hard— our crowd had no romantic illusions about heroin, and cocaine wasn't really available. Hallucinogens were the big attraction, along with marijuana and hashish. I was eager to get in on it all. Since Jock was already of an age when such experimentation came naturally, I only had to stay close to get a head start.

December 1971—Christmas break. I was thirteen, a grade eight student. Jock, his best friend Mike, and I pooled our meagre funds and sent Jock down to the pool hall. His mission: to buy some pot, something we had yet to try. Jock came back a couple of hours later. "I couldn't find any pot," he said, "but I got these." In his hand were several little packets. It was LSD, a variety the seller had described as "purple microdot." We took them.

I still don't know if that was the best LSD ever or whether the effect was just amplified by my youth and inexperience, but it was certainly overwhelming. We put on an appropriate record—Pink Floyd's *Ummagumma*—and waited for the stuff to kick in. It didn't really hit till partway through King Crimson's *Lizard*. Then, liftoff. None of us could talk for a while, a function of brains racing with inexpressible thoughts. Stupid and nonsensical thoughts, most likely, but understood at the time as profundities too awe-inspiring for mere speech. I recall constantly brushing at some sort of red bead curtain that seemed to hang in front of me. At one point I had the sudden conviction that my arm was going to eat my head.

It's hard to recommend LSD as an alternative to summer camp, but it seems to me now just another part of my adolescence, alongside more prosaic activities like playing sports or watching TV. It isn't heroin or crack—those relentless hobbies will turn you into a frantic mother bird with a nest full of gaping mouths. LSD and other hallucinogens—my brother and I would eventually try a few— were more like a series of self-contained experiences that picked you up and dropped you off about eight hours later, sated. At about five bucks a pop, once every three or six months, LSD did not require any of us to steal TV sets.

Nor was it the end of childhood innocence or the beginning of a jaded and premature adulthood—it was an artificially induced experience of wonder. My use of hallucinogens ran its course by the time I was seventeen. It would have ended one hit sooner, but one night at a party some acid-happy friends stuck half a tab into a Pop Tart and fed it to me. They did have the decency to explain the situation immediately. With about eight or nine beers under my belt, I didn't believe their story— until, in a remarkable demonstration of the drug's power, the drunkenness slid away, as if the LSD had simply taken me by the collar and lifted me above the fog. It would be my final trip. And my final Pop Tart.

Later I would learn first-hand that any kind of contraband drug use carried dangers. You never really knew what you were buying. On at least two occasions, my attempts to buy powdered mescaline led me to something that turned out to be, in all likelihood, PCP, a.k.a. "angel dust"—a substance whose one-time popularity remains an enduring mystery to me. We used to call it "horse tranquilizer." Consuming it was always an accident, like getting food poisoning at a restaurant. PCP produced a feeling rather like being drunk and sober simultaneously—stupid, slow, and sloppy, yet without the blissful oblivion of alcoholic intoxication. You remained perfectly aware of your disgusting condition. It's horrible stuff, sold in the guise of various other products. Powder in tin foil looks like powder—there's not much quality control in the street-drug business.

Mom and Dad would not have agreed with my assessment of LSD's relative harmlessness. Although they did not find out about the acid-dropping until many years later, there was one near-miss. A friend and I dropped some acid one Saturday, expecting it to run its course by dinnertime. Whether because we started too late or because the dose in question proved too powerful, we miscalculated. And so I found myself sitting at the family dinner table while still firmly planted in Strangeville. It's a nightmarish scenario for any young acidhead. As count-less hipster films have suggested, the everyday world of the North American family dinner becomes a surreal and somewhat horrifying experience when one is under the effects of LSD. The quotidian seems absurd, and in the complete absence of hunger (acid works on the appetite in a way almost exactly opposite of marijuana) food can appear both ludicrous and vile. Stifling the urge to laugh at amusements no one else will perceive is a struggle. Worst of all is the paranoia that results from the complete inability to judge the suitability of your own behaviour. Then, once your odd demeanour has attracted suspicion, your saucer-like dilated pupils are there to confirm it.

The real giveaway was the cutlery. I couldn't manage it. Throughout dinner I repeatedly threw down my knife and fork with loud sighs of frustration. "May I be excused?" I barked.

In the resulting silence I scurried down the stairs. Not cool.

My parents came downstairs and went into the base-ment den. They almost never did that. I headed up the stairs, making for the back door and freedom. Too late. "Steve," Dad's voice intoned, "can we speak to you for a minute?"

My parents, I felt sure, were not well-versed in drug culture. They'd have read scary stories in newspapers and *Newsweek* magazine, certainly. But even if Dad read that Timothy Leary book his psychiatrist gave him, I don't think he really grasped the pharmaceutical foundations of those psychedelic prayers.

I needed a story, something plausible that would take the heat off. There had been occasions recently when Les-lie's friends had popped Wake-Up pills, over-the-counter amphetamines, for a cheap buzz. I decided to offer that up as my explanation.

They bought it. And were devastated. Wake-Up pills! Our son! My relief at having sold the story was tempered by a new realization of just how appalled they would be to discover the truth.

LSD is not addictive, but my experiences demonstrate just which intoxicants are most likely to play hell with your life if encountered at an impressionable age. Not long before the LSD incident, in that same family basement at 54 Clement Drive, I got drunk for the first time.

It was that same 1971 Christmas break, and this time I was in the basement with Jock and my friend Bodo. With Jock's help we had obtained a bottle of something called Calona Double Jack. It cost $1.05 and went equally badly with meat or fish. One moment I was sitting on the floor guzzling, the next I had somehow ended up flat on my back, knocking over a set of chess pieces, laughing like a hyena. A pivotal moment, like a rat running his first maze.

THE TIME WOULD come when alcohol would cause me a great many problems. But the path to delinquency wasn't that simple. There were other motivations. For a gangly kid entering junior high, getting into trouble could be a means of survival.

Every kid on the brink of the adolescent abyss seeks a strategy for ensuring safety and rank. Those who lack physical strength and athletic prowess will often find themselves terrorized and humiliated. Social status offers protection—physical protection, where boys are concerned. You need to make alliances. Not long after we moved to 54 Clement I began to feel a desperate need for protection.

I made a friend in class. Reid, the son of an RCMP officer, lived a block away from us. He was a small kid with a shock of Beatle-ish black hair and narrow, squinty eyes behind thick black-framed glasses. Somehow he managed to rock that look. For an unusually small boy, Reid was possessed of an eerie self-confidence. We bonded over music. He was a fanatic about identifying clues to the "Paul is dead" controversy, ranging from the obvious— Paul McCartney facing backward on the back of the *Sgt. Pepper's* cover—to the truly obscure, like a Canadian-only Beatles release called *Very Together* that featured a photo of four candles, one recently extinguished. We would sit in Reid's living room, pore over the clues, and try to get his turntable to run backward.

Reid often spoke about his previous address on the east side of Brandon. It was a tougher neighbourhood, with more famous thugs—in particular, Eddie Houle. I once encountered Houle's gang at a hockey game, practising random terror on bystanders, then on me after I made the mistake of attempting a pleasantry. Suck-ups are to be punished. Eddie and his boys chased me to a bus stop and surrounded me. At the last moment I was spared a beating when one of their gang turned out to be a schoolmate, who vouched for me. But before the bus arrived Eddie stepped close. "You think you're safe now?" he hissed. Then he kicked me three times, hard and remarkably fast.

Reid claimed he was pals with those guys. Anybody that messed with him would have to tangle with Eddie.

Reid had plans of a criminal nature. He had spotted a potato chip truck that was habitually parked a few blocks away, and he wanted to break into it. That never came off, though it probably inspired another caper later that year that involved lying in wait for milk trucks. When the driver left the truck idling we would open the back doors and steal plastic milk jugs, redeemable for forty cents each. Our downfall: redeeming the jugs at the same grocery store the truck had been idling behind. The second time we tried it, another milk truck swung in behind, blocking the lane. A sting! We were busted. My parents were horrified.

Meanwhile my biggest problems would come from a plan I didn't even join.

Shortly after our family moved into 54 Clement one of us kids made a weird discovery. Hidden in the rafters of the furnace room was a bottle of chloroform and a pile of new syringes. It lent credence to vague rumours about the eccentricity of the previous tenants. One of that family's teenagers had carried the nickname "Rigor Mortis"—a sort of Goth girl before her time. What anyone would do with chloroform and syringes was, and is still, a mystery to me. But someone else had ideas.

I showed the strange discovery to Reid and another school buddy named Darryl. Mistake. Reid's squinty eyes lit up. "Let's take this stuff out," he said, "and inject some cats."

I liked cats. We had one. I voted no. Reid and Darryl voted yes, and took the chloroform and syringes with them. I was in a panic. One did not rat on friends, but this seemed to me beyond the pale. I told Mom. Parents were called, which in the case of Reid meant notifying the RCMP. Suddenly I had two more enemies at school.

One day while out riding my bike, I found myself circled. Reid led the little biker group, swooping around on his little Mustang banana-seat two-wheeler. "C'mon Steve," Reid sneered. "Don't be a chump."

"Why'd you rat us out, Steve?" Darryl asked.

"I'm going to put in a call to Eddie Houle," Reid said. "You'll be dead."

There was a protocol for after-school fighting. An actual fight, agreed upon by both parties, would happen only if the antagonists were roughly the same size and skill level. Otherwise, violence was more a matter of bullying and intimidation. An alpha tough guy might decide to make your life Hell, and Hell it would become. I had been in a few fights—it was inevitable. Generally I did okay, since there wouldn't have been a fight if I was up against a real scrapper. It was strange, though—even if I held my own, I would be scared of the other kid afterward. Fighting terrified me. It represented chaos. Anything could happen.

I lacked instruction in self-defence. Dad certainly wasn't teaching me to fight, and there were no *Karate Kid* movies on TV—only *The Three Stooges*. Had I been a little more worldly, exposed to just a little bit of Eastern culture, I might have made something out of that influence. Perhaps some sort of hybrid Stooge martial art—a crane stance, a mantis position, two fingers in the eye, a double ear pull, and a *woop woop woop woop woop.*

But I never attempted to hone any kind of fighting skill. Physical combat requires confidence. I was confident only in the potential for defeat and humiliation.

Ordinarily, Reid and I might have been legitimate combatants—I was bigger, but with a complete lack of skill or coordination, which evened things out. Reid wasn't having any of that, though. He played Boss Tiny, whose commands are executed by henchmen. He carried off his kingpin act with a certain panache. Vincent Massey now seemed to me very hostile territory. I pleaded with my parents to take me out of Vincent Massey and send me back to J.R. Reid. They agreed reluctantly. It was only pushing the problem down the road. There was no grade eight at J.R. Reid. The next year it would be Massey again.

My first day of grade eight—all the students were in the gym, being assigned to homerooms. I scanned the room nervously, looking for Reid. The "Bs" came up early, and my homeroom assignment was made. Next, "C." Suddenly I was no longer worried about locating Reid. I had other problems. A familiar name had just been added to my homeroom. My new classmate shambled over to where I was standing and threw me a sideways grin. I knew him. His name was Al C. This looked like very big trouble.

Al was a local legend. His fame as a thug had spread beyond his own elementary school, Earl Oxford, and reached my own. In one of those mysterious schoolyard grapevine reports, it had become common knowledge at J.R. Reid that Al was "after me." "Saw your friend Al C. today," another student would joke. Why Al was "after me" was never articulated. As far as I could recall, we had never met. But we were used to those kind of mysteries. A guy like Al didn't need an excuse. He had it in for me, that's all. Everyone knew it.

Now we were together. Not just the same grade—the same class. And not just Al, but his buddy Ron F. too. Grade eight was going to be worse than I'd feared.

But Al did not torment me. On the contrary—he seemed to be seeking me out, offering a mumbling sort of conversation as he slouched down the halls. It became clear that Al did not bear me any ill will. The old rumours had never been true. In fact, Al told me, he had seen me around town and thought I looked pretty cool. Moreover we found plenty of common ground. Al may have been tough, but he was no knuckle-dragger. He turned out to be highly intelligent, with a penchant for observation, a sense of the absurd, and a cynical sense of humour. We shared tastes and opinions. When *Rolling Stone* magazine said the new Rolling Stones album *Exile on Main Street* was a bad record, Al and I both knew they were full of shit (as they later admitted). Physically we looked a matched set, both sporting the same shaggy, shoulder-length dirty-blonde hair. We were buddies.

I never did find out whether Reid got in touch with his pal Eddie. That was no longer an issue.

Was my new alliance cynical? An arrangement of convenience? Sure, friendship with Al had its practical side. It offered protection. But it didn't feel like a calculated move—Al and I seemed to click.

Yet I was always aware of a fundamental difference between us. While I was a kid from an apple-pie household, dipping my toe into delinquency, Al came by his inner turmoil honestly. His mom had died young, and his father had married a woman with a young son of her own. Al and his stepmom were not on good terms. Entering grade eight, he already had a long juvenile record and his very own probation officer. Sometimes when we got drunk he wanted to beat me up, but only rarely. It was a small price to pay. Nobody messed with us. And if hanging with Al meant boozing and trouble, well, I was headed down that track anyway.

The milk-truck heist had been a start. It had been followed by a bust for shoplifting an Alice Cooper album (*Killer*) from K-Mart. Dad had to attend juvenile court with me. Experts say it's important for families to do things together, but I think it's possible to overstate the benefits.

Grade eight marked a sharp break from my scholastic past. My marks sucked. I was a regular in the principal's office. As far as I was concerned, it was working out great: my fears of being bullied had not materialized. Rather, I was on the winning team. But once again my stretch at Vincent Massey would be brief. This time, leaving wasn't my idea.

I was never formally expelled. At a meeting called by Principal Henderson, it was strongly suggested to my parents that I be sent elsewhere for the good of all concerned. On my last day I took the opportunity to plant a snowball between the shoulder blades of Mr. Haddad, my French teacher. He hauled me down to the office, but

Henderson could only shrug. "I'd expel him, but..." It was a free shot.

They put me in a school located in another town. I began commuting thirty-three miles to school every day, hitching a ride with a teacher.

But I was still hanging with Al and company on weekends. The level of transgression escalated. Al, Ron F., another young hoodlum, and I would be busted for a series of break-and-enters. There were busts for marijuana and liquor. My parents came to dread the sound of a telephone ringing after midnight.

One day an RCMP officer came to the door, asking questions about a drug raid the previous night. A hash pipe had been found in my buddy Gord's apartment. They could charge you with possession of cannabis just for the bits of resin caked inside the pipe. Gord had immediately ratted me out. Not as reprehensible as it sounds—he had already done time in jail for drug trafficking, and claiming ownership of that pipe would have sent him away again.

For my mother the immediate problem posed by the officer's visit was that my Grandma was visiting at the time. Mom quietly asked if the officer would mind going around to the back door and sneaking into the basement, which he graciously agreed to do. I ended up charged with drug possession. But at least Grandma never found out.

The drinking escalated too. By the time I reached grade eleven, I was a confirmed problem drinker. Had I ever been found beaten to death in an alley, I could fairly have been described to the press as "a figure known to police."

Although I made the usual efforts to disguise my activities, it was clear to all that I was off the rails. My parents struggled to find the appropriate response. At one point they threatened to send me to a strict private academy in Winnipeg. After I set another family first by failing grade ten mathematics—I missed over forty classes that year—they swallowed hard, abandoned their principles, and offered me a bribe. Noting my growing interest in photography, they offered to buy me an expensive camera should I pass grade eleven with a B average. It worked, but they still felt bad about it. They had never imagined it would be necessary to bribe their son to do something he should be doing for the sake of his own future.

It wasn't often that something snapped. But it happened. One night my friends and I were playing cards in the basement. Mom had to work early the next day and had asked us to keep the noise down. We didn't. She came downstairs again and asked us to pack it in. I argued with her—I'm pretty sure I had been drinking. Mom was reduced to tears. The card game continued.

Next day I came home to find Dad standing in the dining room. "I am going to knock your teeth down your throat," he said.

Dad was the kind of guy who couldn't even curse convincingly—once or twice I heard him try to say "fuck," and it just sounded wrong, like a suburban white kid trying to sound street. This was the first time I had ever heard him threaten serious violence. To his credit, he sounded convincing. Without a word I turned on my heel and headed right back out the door. A few friends took up a collection so I could spend the night in a motel. By the next day tempers had cooled, and we were both apologetic. Hardly a fair trade, apologetically speaking. Dad was the kind of Christian who would apologize to a lion for being chewy.

My career as a juvenile delinquent was cruising along smoothly. Then, a tactical mistake—my eighteenth birthday. From now on my crimes would be dealt with in adult court. And so it came to pass, very quickly.

12

TRIALS

G AVIN WAS my best friend in high
school. He was the son of a fellow
United Church minister, who was a good friend of Dad's.
Gavin and I were sensitive souls who liked to drink beer
under the stars, lying on the hood of his '55 Ford pick-
up, discussing Dostoevsky and girls. But when it came
to the law we were gleeful little cynics. Gavin and I were
fully aware that maximum penalties for juvenile offences
topped out at twenty-five-dollar fines. Being under eighteen was like having diplomatic immunity. All very well,
until I had that one birthday too many. My adult criminal record began with a charge of carrying open liquor
in public, laid at approximately 12:20 a.m. on August 26,
1976. A mere appetizer.

One fall night Al, Gavin, and I were at a local 7-Eleven
after returning from a football game in Winnipeg. We
were a little drunk, but by our own high standards not
particularly. Al started raising hell—he broke a bottle of

salad dressing on the floor of the store and then added an overripe banana. I stole some tinned oysters. Police were summoned.

Answering the call was Officer B., a cop with a history of aggressive policing. Al could be obnoxious—we all could. From my current vantage point, I might be inclined to punch my younger self in the throat. It's an idea that seems to have occurred to others as well.

Officer B. and his partner decided to tow Al's car. Al argued—the store manager had agreed to let him park the car there overnight. Al was standing by the squad car, making his case. Officer B. suddenly popped like an IED. Grabbing Al by his long, dirty-blonde hair, Officer B. jammed a knee into his abdomen and stuffed him into the squad car.

Al thrust the car keys through the open window of the car. "Gavin," he called, "take the car and drive it away."

Gavin took the keys, and looked nervously at Officer B. "Any reason I can't do that?" he asked.

Officer B. replied with a sweeping kick that took Gavin's legs out from under him. Slapping handcuffs on one of his wrists, he pulled the cuffs up while bringing his knee down on Gavin's chest. He stuffed Gavin into the back seat with Al and then came toward me. Another sweep kick, and I was on the pavement.

We were not the only ones caught off guard by Officer B.'s violent outburst. His partner also seemed at a bit of a loss. After I regained my feet, the other cop pushed me around a bit. "Gonna keep causing trouble?" he muttered. But there wasn't much conviction to it. His real goal, it seemed, was to distract me from Officer B.'s rampage.

At last the officers drove off with Al and Gavin. I was left standing in the parking lot.

Gavin and Al were both charged and released. Later, filled with righteous outrage, Gavin and I recounted the sequence of events to our parents. We yelped about law-suits. "You provoke them," Dad said. "You're putting yourself in those situations."

Still the police reaction disturbed them. And since I hadn't been arrested, what point could there have been in knocking me down?

The same question apparently occurred to the police. Three months after the incident an official report was filed. The three of us, it claimed, had physically attacked the officers, who were then forced to defend themselves. I was now facing five charges, including assault of a police officer and obstruction of justice.

Gavin and Al were juveniles. I testified for Gavin in juvenile court. The presiding judge dismissed my testimony as concocted. Gavin was convicted and assigned the usual modest fine and probation. Al left the country, thumbing his way south. My case was different. I was eighteen—an adult. A trial date was set. These were serious charges. If convicted I was looking at potential jail time. The days of shoplifting Alice Cooper records now seemed like the innocent idylls of youth.

A couple of months before the trial I received a letter from Canada Customs and Immigration, asking me to attend a meeting. At the appointed time I was ushered into an office containing a desk and a bureaucrat. He flipped through a file while I sat, still waiting to find out what was up. "You were born in Ohio, correct?" he asked.

He continued to flip through the file. "Ah," he said, "I see here that your father exercised his right to bring you into the country as a Canadian citizen."

And with that, our business was done. This meeting, it turned out, had been the commencement of a possible deportation proceeding. Someone in the police department or prosecutor's office had checked my birth certificate and informed immigration authorities that I was a potentially dangerous alien. Presumably the plan was to drive me to the North Dakota border and dump me. It would have been a dicey situation. My initial one-and-a-half years in Ohio had not allowed much time for networking, and I certainly lacked contacts in Fargo or Bismarck. I could have built some sort of snow shelter, close to the border where my folks could lob food to me across the line.

I got to stay in the country. But these guys weren't fooling around. Perhaps not surprising, since the case boiled down to we said/they said. If our version was judged true, the police were officially liars.

Among the most remarkable aspects of the story, in hindsight, is that my parents truly believed me. For years I had been putting them through the wringer with drunkenness, truancy, and petty delinquency. But they knew me. And this time they believed me.

Or is that simply what parents do?

Neil Entwhistle's mom believed in him. Entwhistle was a Brit living in Massachusetts. In January 2006 he shot his wife and baby daughter and immediately jumped on a flight to the U.K., where police eventually found him at his parents' place in Nottinghamshire. He claimed to have been so overwhelmed at discovering his dead family that he simply had to flee the country. According to Entwhistle's mom, her son is innocent.

In the summer of 2009 Ryan Jenkins killed his ex-wife Jasmine in L.A. and then took off for B.C., where he hanged himself in a motel room. His parents insist that Jenkins was innocent of the murder.

Now I cringe every time some devoted mother pops up on the evening news proclaiming that her misunderstood son could never be guilty of murdering his wife, despite the video surveillance footage and "My husband did it" scrawled on the floor in the victim's own blood. I marvel anew at the parental capacity for self-delusion. At the time of my trial I knew that my parents' belief in me would probably inspire that same brand of skepticism.

Dave, one of Mom's co-workers at the community college, had some pals on the police force. He teased my mother for her faith in me. My friends and I, Dave explained, were lying little troublemakers. When she recounted the conversation later, Mom seethed. Perhaps more than anything else about the period, I remember her anger. After all I had done to Mom and Dad, how humbling.

Was it parental blindness, inspired by love? No. I really was innocent—of these charges, at least—and my parents knew it. I think they knew I couldn't lie so convincingly. And, sorely though I tested it, they had faith in me.

My parents hired a good lawyer and we prepared for our day in court. Just before the trial began our lawyer sat us down and revealed that the prosecution had made an offer—in effect, a guarantee that no penalty would be sought if I would admit guilt. My lawyer suggested I take a little walk and think before answering. Gavin and I took a stroll through the halls and talked, but there was not much question about it. We were young and filled with the fire of righteousness. I wanted to go ahead with the trial. My parents agreed. Into court we went.

Pretty fascinating stuff, all in all. It was easy to get caught up in the process and forget that I was sitting at the defendant's table. The proceedings were not exactly the sort of legal jousting later glorified on *Law & Order,* et al. At times the trial resembled a political smear campaign more than a fact-finding exercise.

Witnesses were called, including the cops, the store owner, and a few onlookers. I'm not sure my lawyer would have called Al, even if he hadn't fled the country. Gavin didn't testify.

At one point a witness misidentified the kind of car we had been in—which was a green Volkswagen Fastback. I whispered to my lawyer and sat back to await the dramatic debunking. "Are you sure it wasn't a Volkswagen?" my lawyer asked.

The witness insisted it had been a red Austin Mini (a telling mistake—the Mini belonged to a different friend of mine). My lawyer just shrugged. Dramatics may work for television, but a good lawyer doesn't smack the judge over the head.

Eventually my lawyer put me on the stand, where I described the events of the evening. Then, cross examination. To the chagrin of my parents, my lawyer, and myself, I had recently handed the prosecutor a bit of extra ammunition. "Mr. Burgess," the prosecutor asked, "weren't you in court earlier this very week on a charge of drinking and driving?"

I had been indeed. Racing to the store to get more beer before closing time, I was pulled over and flunked a Breathalyzer. A guilty plea, a $250 fine, six-month licence suspension, and a rather inconvenient black mark on my reputation just in time for the big trial. Two court appearances in a single week—a family record that would never be challenged.

"Have you also been arrested for possession of marijuana?" he continued.

Also true, I allowed. "Are you an alcoholic?" he asked.

No, I insisted. I am not. Possibly adding perjury to my growing list of crimes.

He then wound up and delivered his final spitball. "Is it not true," he asked, "that last Tuesday afternoon, you and your friend Gavin were on Princess Avenue, drunk and disorderly, pointing and laughing at a mentally retarded Indian woman?"

Stunned, I paused a moment. Just where had I been last Tuesday? Well, not there, anyway. My subsequent denial was thus emphatic and indignant.

Passing the prosecutor's table, I paused. "You didn't see me do that," I protested.

"I don't know," he said with a grin. "Was it you?"

As my lawyer explained later, "He just wanted the judge to see you thinking about it."

The verdict, when it came, was oddly anticlimactic. Throughout the afternoon the prosecution had attempted to paint me as having been stone drunk that night; in his closing arguments my lawyer suggested that, if so, I was not responsible for my actions. The judge agreed. "There will be an order of acquittal," the judge said.

My lawyer turned to me and smiled. "Stay out of trouble," he said.

I had been found not guilty—not because the judge believed my version of events, but because legally I was judged too drunk to know any better.

Later we heard from a friend of Dad's who also knew the judge. He suggested that the judge was more than familiar with the policing style of Officer B. Had he simply been looking for a legal hook upon which to hang my acquittal? My parents didn't care. I had dodged a bullet.

We all understood that I had been lucky. And as it turned out, that would be the end of my criminal career. But I wasn't out of the woods yet. I was still a drunk.

BY MY EARLY twenties I had embarked upon a career as a disc jockey, spinning 45s in small Canadian towns. My drinking had taken me along that familiar curve from teenage party animal admired for his tremendous capacity, to teenage party animal inspiring a growing level of concern among friends, to twentysomething guy drinking himself out of a job or two, to guy living alone in a strange city and regularly hauling home forty-two beers in a backpack, enough for two solitary trips to Blottotown.

Every drunk has stories. Actor John Larroquette tells of emerging from a blackout to find he was on an airplane and trying to figure out through casual small talk just where it was he was going. I'm not really the best source for some of my own ugly tales; you'd have to ask a participant whose personal think tank was not flooded at the time.

But I remember the life, and the feelings associated with it. There's a sort of romantic fatalism that young people often embrace—"No future," as the Sex Pistols sang. I wallowed in that, for lack of any other option. It did seem as though the future was something for which I would not be eligible.

It's remarkable to consider the things one can be grateful for. My luckiest break may have been losing control of my bladder. After drinking myself senseless, I would often wake up soaked in my own urine. It wasn't pleasant. My penchant to view myself as a complex, self-destructive philosopher/romantic was hard to maintain—the romantic part, at least—when I was busy wetting myself like an untrained mongrel.

My method of dealing with it may provide a perverse glimpse into the problem-solving techniques of an addict. Consider my options: A) Quit drinking, or B) Prepare for each solitary drinking bout by stripping to my undies and then covering the entire apartment floor with newspapers, since there was no telling where I might eventually fall senseless and stain the hardwood. B) it was. I could have sold tickets and made it into a lottery, like cow-patty bingo.

There were other disasters—many. If all of the humiliation, degradation, and failure doesn't make one stop, what will? What epic piece of misadventure will finally be enough? A good question with no answer I could see. As it turned out, drama wouldn't be necessary.

I was parked in my favorite armchair in an Edmonton, Alberta, basement suite. For the last few months I had been working the all-night shift for a local rock station. Overnight shifts were great for a drunk—drink yourself silly the night before and you get plenty of recuperative time before having to go to work. On this occasion I was drinking tequila. It wasn't going down so great, which happened sometimes. The clock hit midnight. It was now April 3, 1983—Easter Sunday.

As I sat, my mind wandered around to a familiar theme—the possibility of quitting. I had never made a serious attempt, afraid that in failure I might come to resemble those buffoons who sit in the bar every afternoon, loudly proclaiming that they are currently consuming their final beer.

A couple of weeks earlier I had met a woman at a party. It had got me thinking of a potential romance. But how? Young women tend to frown on partners who piss themselves in an evening.

Thus even the most routine of happy scenarios ran into a barrier. Sobriety looked like a green pasture on the far side of an electrified prison fence. Still I had long imagined that one day a magical state of readiness would arrive and I would free myself. On that Easter morning I held this belief up to scrutiny. It was horseshit. The fabled day of readiness was like the horizon, perpetually receding as I approached. I had become one of those donkeys with a stick protruding from its halter, from which a carrot dangles—the donkey goes forward, but that clever carrot always escapes.

Sitting in a mustard-yellow armchair in a spare basement suite, I asked myself: Are you ready to quit? The honest answer was no. I did not feel ready.

It led to another logical question: Will you ever be ready? Again, the answer was no. That lovely horizon would always recede. But this realization had a flip side— the understanding that I would never be more ready than I was on that day. If the right day was never coming, then one bad day was as good as any other. It was just a matter of choosing one. So, in my mustard-yellow armchair on Easter morning, I decided to quit drinking. Leaving the tequila bottle on the side table, I went to bed.

In Dickens's *A Christmas Carol*, Scrooge awakes on Christmas morning, realizes he is still in this world rather than dead and unmourned, and breaks into a dance of giddy glee. It's a moment of pure joy. But it passes over a key decision, a moment crucial to Scrooge's trans- formation. What if Scrooge had awakened and, after a moment of confusion teetering between dream and real- ity, shaken off the spell and dismissed the entire vision as a fantastic nightmare? Habit and custom exert a tre- mendous pull. Even a sudden gift of revelation can pop like a soap bubble, leaving the recipient to take up the old, familiar ways.

Drunks have a reflex, developed after countless embar- rassments, that causes a wave of revulsion to strike immediately at the point of regaining consciousness. "Oh my God," thinks the sodden brain, "what did I do last night?" It's as regular as the chimes of Big Ben, even on those occasions when it turns out you actually stayed home and watched Godzilla flicks until you keeled over.

When I awoke late on that Easter morning I did not break into Scrooge's happy dance. Instead the reflex kicked in: "What nonsense was I spouting last night?"

Instinctively I prepared to repudiate the optimistic dreams of the night before. There had been no spirits, except the problematic kind. And it was those distilled spirits of Mexico that had filled my head with visions of a new life. It wouldn't be the first drunken fantasy I'd sobered up and forgotten.

But standing under the shower, I let myself wonder: Suppose I'd meant it? All I really needed to do was take myself seriously. The idea began to take hold. Like many a radical notion, it was a simple one: I could change my life and my fate with a decision.

Remarkably, the issue seemed uncertain for only a few days. A sense of elation and possibility was building, and the momentum proved irresistible. Scrooge's dance would not be denied me—only delayed a little. A few days after Easter I was pulling an overnight shift, all alone in the quiet radio station. Walking out of the studio to clear paper from the clattering news wire, I jumped into the air and slapped the arch of the doorway. I'd done it. I knew I would never drink again. I had cleared the fence running. I was free.

Nothing ever happened with that young woman. She was a *deus ex machina,* a cheap dramatic trick. She was like a giant meteor, dropping in out of nowhere to erase the past, changing everything and vanishing. Most important non-girlfriend ever.

I waited two weeks before telling my parents. I wanted it to seem credible. The happiness and relief in Mom's voice were something I had often dreamed of hearing. I had given her a gift that was long overdue, and had there been any wavering in my resolve it would have disappeared at that moment.

But in fact I had no doubts. I was finished with alcohol. It was gone like an amputated limb. Strange that I should be able to make the break so cleanly when others have struggled—people I've known, before and since, who fight and backslide and try again, always battling. Why me?

For that matter, why did I become a drunk in the first place?

Circumstances certainly didn't set me up for social drinking. Manitoba winters are not cocktail parties. On the weekends we juveniles who were bent on misadventure had to congregate outdoors, hiding from cops while staying out of the wind in clumps of bush or sheds—once, even in the cabs of used combines on a farm implement dealership lot. Get as much alcohol into your belly, as fast as possible, before the cold becomes too much. Keeping the beer on ice was never a problem, at least.

Our music spoke of a more sophisticated world. Van Morrison sang about his "Wild Night": "And all the girls walk by, dressed up for each other / And the boys do the boogie-woogie on the corner of the street..." Nobody wrote pop songs about Manitoba and trying to get drunk before your feet or your beer froze solid. Whatever legacy this social schedule may have left, it certainly inculcated the very worst of drinking habits.

And yet as far as I know my young drinking buddies did not become problem drinkers en masse. Just me. Why?

As a drunk I always suffered from a serious disadvantage. Many dipsomaniacs have horror stories to lean on when explaining their histories. They were abused, or poor, or coat-hangered for smiling, or made into unwilling surrogates for Mommy's failed Broadway ambitions. Not me. I had wonderful parents. In my parent-child relationship the pain flowed pretty much in one direction. I'd kill to have some of the excuses other spongeheads can offer. But it was my curse to have had two loving guardians and a perfectly good upbringing.

I had at least one glimpse of the other side. In 1973 I was just shy of my fifteenth birthday, hanging out with

Al and getting into various types of mischief. My hair was draped over my shoulders, and, inspired by *A Clockwork Orange,* I had taken to wearing a black bowler hat. I was puzzled that so many complete strangers wanted to beat me up.

My parents allowed me to join Al's family on a trip to the West Coast. It would be my first visit. We went to Vancouver, Bowen Island, and up the coast of Vancouver Island to Campbell River. Although I would never have admitted it to myself at the time, I was somewhat awestruck. The citizens of Vancouver and the islands seemed impossibly cool, the weather so agreeably mild, the landscape so full of casual beauty. I resented all that.

Al and I behaved badly, of course. In Campbell River we pelted passersby with ice from our second-storey hotel room. When the desk clerk phoned up to complain, I impersonated the deep voice of Al's father. "No, no," I intoned, "the boys have been right here with me all along..."

But I behaved badly in other ways—shameful ways. I became a profiteer in a family war.

Al and his stepmother were barely civil. The default family dynamic was suppressed hostility. Stepmom, supported by Al's father and protective of her young son, was wary lest my presence tip the balance of power. So she gave me money. Frequently. And I took it. I went shopping at Vancouver record stores, bought myself a Yes *Close to the Edge* T-shirt and a glass hash pipe. Al was seething. "She's trying to buy you off," he would say. I shrugged and counted my war profits.

But I would pay. Al occasionally took out his frustrations by pounding on me. Once when I was lying on a motel room bed he picked up the mattress and launched it into the corner, me with it. I responded by setting off an entire book of matches, which frightened him into letting me out.

Minor beatings were not the worst, though. The worst was the drive back. Over a thousand miles in a massive blue Buick, Al and I in back, the other three up front—a closed container with pressure building steadily. One day Al was teasing his little stepbrother, making him cry. Stepmom snapped. Turning toward the back seat and windmilling her arms at Al, she screamed, "I hate you, I hate you, you son of a bitch!"

Another day, with the Buick barrelling along the highway at seventy mph, Stepmom interrupted another screaming match to point a finger at the corner of the backseat where I was trying to shrink into the upholstery. "Why is *he* always here when we fight?" she shouted.

Believe me, ma'am, I would much rather be strapped to the roof rack like a dead moose.

Brandon. Brandon. BRAN-don. Bran-DON. Bran. Done. The mantra repeated over and over and over in my head as the telephone poles crawled by, the blessed name tumbling and tumbling until the stuffing came out, losing cohesion and dissolving into meaningless syllables. I longed to be home. I had discovered the terror and strangeness of life outside the parental umbrella.

Moreover, I had seen first-hand evidence that my delinquent buddy Al had good reason for acting out. I had no such justification.

If I needed more evidence of my willful perversity I needed only to compare my own upbringing with my mother's.

There's always a tendency to mine one's personal history for justifications. Everybody has pain. But it's not that simple. My mother is proof. If an emotionally troubled childhood led to alcoholism Mom would have been a booze hound, and I would merely have been carrying on a family tradition. As it was my parents never drank at all until I was in my teens. When they did start it was a glass of wine at dinner or a single Scotch. I never saw either one of them even get tipsy. Not for the last time I would see my mother's example defeat the easy explanations.

Why, then? Impossible to know for sure, but I have come to believe it's mostly a matter of personality type. I'm an extremist. Over the years I have seen the same powerful drive, the same obsessive impulse that made me a determined drunk reappearing in more benign and even useful areas, such as a consuming interest in photography or travel. For good or ill my approach tends toward the all or nothing.

If I can't blame Mom and Dad for my drinking problem, perhaps I can thank them for the clean finality of its resolution. I am pretty sure I know which side of the family provided the meat cleaver with which I separated a troubled past from a brighter future. She who had sat on dark cellar stairs years ago, unwilling to yield to a powerful force, forming resolutions that would shape and change her future—she passed on to me the weapon that I finally laid hands on.

April 3, 1983, was the beginning. It was renewal and redemption. For a couple of years afterward I experienced something like the opposite of mild depression—I awoke every day thinking myself lucky to open my eyes with no evil to reflect on from the night before. I felt I was starting the race fifty yards down the track from the rest of the pack. And part of my incandescent little ball of personal joy was the frequent reminder that my parents were proud of me, that I had finally started the long process of payback for all the fear and worry. In years to come we would spend all our Christmases together, happy times heightened just a little by the unspoken pleasure of our changed circumstances.

I knew that Mom was thrilled and happy. She made that clear. And yet she would never completely leave those days behind. Every so often, largely through my own thoughtlessness, I would see the proof.

The awful truth is that the life of a young delinquent is mostly fun. You don't have to worry about paying rent. Your actions may cause you problems with the law, but juvenile penalties are light. As long as you're still at home it's party time. Most of the stress is experienced by your parents. Which is something young jerks don't seem to care much about at the time.

Roxanne was another of my old drinking pals, one of the few from the old bush crew with whom I had subsequently maintained a friendship. A successful massage therapist, she would sometimes stop by the house to say hello. Roxanne would eventually become one of the very few people I ever knew my mother to actively despise.

I really don't know whether Rox was trying to upset my mother, or whether she just had an unconscious genius for pushing the biggest, reddest buttons. One day, when Mom was doing some yard work, Rox was passing by and stopped to reminisce. "We used to have some big parties in that basement. This was the party house, all right. What were you guys thinking? Your kids got away with murder."

As my mother described the conversation to me, I saw her as angry as I can ever recall. And it wasn't that Mom thought Rox was being unfair in her assessment. Mom agreed with her. Roxanne was like a thief who takes advantage of your unlocked door and then returns to crap on your rug. For the rest of Mom's life, my teenage troubles left her convinced she had been a failure as a guardian.

I don't know what my parents could have done—five kids in six years with all the resultant issues to be juggled, plus two careers and at least one seriously rogue element dragging them into uncharted legal territory. What to do? Would that private school offering quasi-military discipline have helped? Who knows? I'm glad they didn't follow through on that. But I know Mom wrestled with those decisions. I know she never stopped.

Once at a family reunion I made the mistake of reminiscing about some youthful criminal episode accomplished with my pals. Mom abruptly left the room. Even years later in the apartment at Riverheights Terrace, after I discovered that one of the home care nurses had been a high school classmate of mine and we started talking about teenage hijinks, we were interrupted by Mom's whispery voice. "Could you change the subject?" she said. "It upsets me."

She was in her eighties by then—more than three decades removed from the events in question. Carefree delinquency is no victimless crime.

13

WHO KILLED GRANDMA?

M Y STINT at an Edmonton radio station coincided almost perfectly with the Gretzky Era. I was in the stands in 1985 when the Oilers beat Philly for their second Cup. I would witness the metastasis of the West Edmonton Mall from a somewhat-larger-than-ordinary shopping centre into a thing with dolphins and submarines and its own tidal forces. I would be there for the rise and fall of Culture Club, would play the early hits of Madonna and the hit of A Flock of Seagulls. My shaggy-rugged basement suite was on the south side of town in the district of Petrolia, which promised to be charming someday when the runty little trees grew in. Grandma's neighbourhood was just about as far across town as it could be. All the same, we were neighbours. Of all Annie Slorance's grandchildren, only I could be reached by a local call. I was, literally, her closest relative. Karma can be a bitch.

One day in sunny Petrolia I sat at my fold-up kitchen

table, chatting on the phone. No sooner had I hung up when the phone rang again. "Hello!" said a cheery woman. "Is this Mr. Burgess?"

It was. "Oh! I have been trying to get you on the phone forever. I called and called for about half an hour! But the phone was busy."

"Talking to a friend," I explained.

"That's nice, isn't it?" the cheerful woman said. "Nice to have friends! It's hard to find the time, frankly. Life can get so busy! But it's nice to have friends like that. Young people are so sociable these days. Always talking on the phone! I envy you. I think it really helps to have a lot of friends to talk to. Just great.

"Anyway," she concluded, "your grandmother's dead."

Later I would wonder whether the cheery nurse employed the same phone technique with every newly bereaved relative, or whether she had inferred my attitude toward Grandma from the infrequency of my visits. There had been exactly two over the previous year. But it's not like Grandma had noticed the lack. By that time she was not even sufficiently aware to be annoyed.

Grandma's independence in the old house on 96th Street had come to an end one day after a final social outing. A friend had escorted her back home, shuffling her carefully into the living room and down onto a comfy green chair. The next day when a nurse came to call she was in the same chair, sitting in her own filth. She had sat there, unable to rise, for almost twenty-four hours.

Grandma was moved to a nursing home. The house was sold. After it was cleaned I ended up getting that green chair, which, all things considered, might have made Grandma happy.

On my first visit to the nursing home Grandma was wheeled out to see me. "It's Steve, Grandma," I said.

"Eh... he's not here," she said. "Do you know him?"

"Yes," I replied. "I'll tell him you said hi."

That went rather well, I thought.

The final visit was oddly upbeat. Staff members informed me that Grandma was convinced she was running for prime minister. They ushered me into the room where she lay in bed. "Hello, Grandma," I said.

"Are you a member of the community?" she asked.

I stammered a few greetings. She watched me with a mischievous smile that was genuinely unsettling. "Well," I said, "guess I'll go now, Grandma."

She raised her eyebrows. "Good luck," she said playfully.

I had the unnerving sense of being gently mocked.

Back before she needed my vote, Grandma was less inclined to cater to my feelings. On those occasions when relatives came to Edmonton—my mother, my Uncle Stan, or my brother Jock whom she loved so dearly—it took strenuous argument to convince Grandma that I should be spared a little face time too. "But Grandma," Jock would plead, "I don't come out from Ontario very often, and Steve is my brother."

"No... eh... well... you see him at Christmas sometimes. This is my visit."

Jock could manage to fight his way across town for a few hours. But if I wanted to see Uncle Stan I had to go to Grandma's house. She would not share her only son with the likes of me.

Stan was my favourite uncle—an animated, genial jester always brimming with astonished admiration for the charms and abilities of his nieces and nephews. We even had the same birthday. But Grandma brought out the worst in him. Watching the two of them was like a case study in sublimated rage. I once had a front-row seat to one of their rhetorical bouts. Stan's face and neck turned a deep, frightening crimson as he rose from his chair and shouted his position. Grandma set her quivering jaw, maintaining her opposition with a mien of injured dignity. Stan crossed the room, stuck his face inches from hers, and screamed: "T-bone! They are T-bone, Mother!"

"Sirloin," Grandma huffed.

They were arguing about what kind of steaks were in the downstairs freezer.

Stan lived in New Jersey and worked in New York. Margaret was in Ottawa. "Joan really spent the most time with our mother," Margaret says. "She was the closest to her."

Joan turned fifty that year. Her red hair was well into its transformation—the bright red was fading as a clean winter white blended in. The transitory result ought to be bottled and sold. Her hair was a light, subtle auburn, kept short but full. She was slender, as always. Her style was elegant, favouring long cloth coats and sometimes a kerchief on a windy day.

Strangely there seem to be no photos from the summer of 1976—strange, because it was a travelling season. Joan had agreed to accompany her mother across the Atlantic on a jumbo jet. Grandma was determined to make a pilgrimage back to her hometown. In the first week of July they embarked for Heathrow and eventually Hawick, Scotland, the border town where young Joan Barron had grown up and where her siblings still lived. "Here I am in Hawick," Mom wrote to us. "Please save my letters because they will serve as a partial record of my trip."

It had been my mother's first time on a 747 and she sounds excited as a schoolgirl. "Simply huge... There were banks of three seats running down each side and a section of four seats down the middle. We were served dinner and breakfast. We also saw a full-length movie

(*Lucky Lady* with Liza Min[n]elli, Burt Reynolds, and Gene Hackman)... We flew over the Pole and because it is July it stayed bright as day all night..."

"Heathrow is not a very well-designed airport. We just caught our flight to Edinburgh with no time to spare. Mom got very tired and upset..."

They arrived on July 5. "The trip to Hawick was beautiful—lovely hilly countryside, green fields and trees, long lines of stone fences called dikes. Hawick is nestled among the hills—you don't see it until you're right on top of it."

They would stay with Grandma's sister Kate at a stone house called Langhurst, set atop a steep hill. Mom was finally meeting aunts she'd only heard stories about. She seems delighted with eighty-one-year-old Liz. "Mom gets pretty angry at Liz," she writes. "Aunt Liz is quite a gossip and doesn't mind dragging all the family gossip out of the closet, and that really annoys Mom... she really is quite rude to her at times."

They drove the countryside in a rental car, various aunts in tow. "Roads are so winding you rarely get above thirty-five or forty. Aunt Belle enjoys it because she rarely gets out and of course Aunt Liz loves it."

Kate, Mom writes on July 15, is "not like the others. Mom really doesn't like her at all. She's very abrupt and short of patience. I get along just fine with her... She prefers us to keep out of her way."

Mom's letters are peppered with reminders for Dad—don't forget the car registration, etc.—and expressions of concern. "I was sorry to hear about Ron's aunt," she writes. "He'll be feeling pretty down."

If constant proximity to Grandma was driving her insane, she did not complain. But she was trapped in the Barron family dynamic, and by July 16 the strain was beginning to show. "I'll be home two weeks from today and that seems like such a long time … It's really difficult to stay around the house because you really feel you're in the way and not wanted. Atmosphere is very tense. We lose the car next Thursday and we're dreading it because we've no way of getting out."

The hill in front of the house was too steep for Grandma. "There are a lot of places I'd like to walk around but I cannot because Mom can't walk and doesn't like me leaving her at all."

On the seventeenth: "I wish I was home. I'm really counting the days until I get there."

On the nineteenth: "Enjoy myself when we're out but hate it at the house. Aunt Kate was particularly nasty to Mom and Aunt Liz last night … She's a very hostile person. She's okay with me but I really find her treatment of Mom and Aunt Liz intolerable."

My mother was defending her mother. It's there in the letters, and in the very fact of the trip itself—Joan Burgess loves her mother. It's a thankless task, and while my mother could not escape it she knew what she was up against.

"She is a dry well," Mom once said. "I have to keep telling myself it's useless to keep trying to get something she doesn't have to give."

Nonetheless, whether it was love, duty, or a combination, when Grandma began her terminal decline it would be her middle child who answered the call. Expecting gratitude would have been unwise.

Toward the end of 1985 there was a momentous development in Alberta politics. Long-time Conservative premier Peter Lougheed announced he would step aside. Transfers of power can make for nervous times in one-party states—something similar had happened a few years earlier when Leonid Brezhnev died and Yuri Andropov took over as Soviet leader. Alberta's new strongman was

Don Getty. Grandma had loved Peter Lougheed, and she was uncomfortable about the change. It didn't help that the eighty-eight-year-old was also losing her grip on reality. It was at this point that Mom came to Edmonton to see Grandma through a medical crisis.

Mom barely had time to visit with me on that trip. She was across town, acting as a full-time nurse and chaperone. One afternoon she returned to the house on 96th with a load of groceries to find Grandma fixing her with a gimlet eye. "I know where you've been," Grandma said.

"Out shopping, Mom," my mother replied.

"No. You've been out talking with them. Scheming."

"Talking to whom, Mom?"

"I know—you're meeting with them. Now that Premier Lougheed is gone they think they can get my money."

"Who, Mom? Who do you mean?"

"The NDP! I know! They want my money but they won't get it!"

Grandma had never approved of my mother's politics.

As her iron grip weakened, money became an increasingly important lever for Grandma. There were regular threats to change her will. And during one of my mother's visits she raised another issue: "What about the piano?"

Decades earlier my grandparents had bought a piano for our family. The girls took lessons but never approached the level where they would have been forced to pronounce "Rachmaninoff" correctly. Dad eventually donated the piano to the church. Forgotten by all, except one. Grandma noted it silently, filing the grievance away with the rest. Now the system was breaking down— files were flying open, disgorging their contents willynilly. "You owe me the money for that piano," Grandma demanded.

She got it, down to the penny, followed by almost every gift she'd ever given us, boxed up and mailed back to Edmonton just as fast as Mom could box and mail. My mother wept over that.

It was 1987 when I finally received that cheery phone call. In hindsight my status as her only local relative might have led to some suspicious questions. Who killed Grandma? Who had the opportunity, and lots and lots of motive? There I was. But no flatfoots inquired.

Actually, if it were up to me Grandma might still be alive. On paper, at least. Recent news reports out of Japan suggest an intriguing option I had failed to consider.

Japanese citizens are renowned for their long lifespans. As of 2009 the country was home to over forty thousand centenarians. But in the case of 113-year-old Fusa Furuya, the issue of life and death turned out to be a little more vague. Furuya was identified as Japan's oldest woman, registered as living with her daughter in Tokyo. However, according to *Jiji Press,* when someone got around to checking up, Furuya's daughter revealed that she hadn't actually seen her mother in approximately fifty years. Other examples emerged, such as Kazuo Tashiro of Tokyo, officially 102 years old, but actually missing since the early seventies. Worst of all was the case of Sogen Kato. When Tokyo officials arrived to help him celebrate his 111th birthday they discovered Kato's mummified remains in his bedroom. Relatives claimed he had shut himself up three decades earlier in hopes of becoming a living Buddha. Pension payments totalling $109,000 U.S. had been credited to Kato's account during that period— recent withdrawals had been made. A living Buddha has no need of earthly money.

I had missed an opportunity. As her only Edmonton relative in those days, I could have easily enough kept Grandma legally viable.

Finally in the news: local resident Joan "Annie" Slorance, 114 years young today. Grandson Steve Burgess says: "She's doing great. Can't come to the phone right now—lot of candles to blow out, you know. Hey, is there any prize money for being the oldest woman in town? Could you look into that?"

My friend and co-worker Tom used to say, "Doesn't it ever occur to anyone that some of those bitter, lonely old people had it coming?"

Not my grandmother, though. She had friends; she had relatives who loved her, irrespective of a grandson's contempt. In spite of everything, the funeral of Joan "Annie" Slorance filled up some pews. Family would shortly begin flying in, including my Uncle Stan and Aunt Margaret. On the day of the funeral Margaret would remain in bed with a migraine.

The minister who presided at the service had never met my grandmother. But it would seem he had done some homework. He had a delicate line to walk, and he walked it like a Flying Wallenda. "Where Joan is now, she understands and forgives everything. And," the minister added gently, "she asks for your forgiveness too."

Both my mother and my uncle began sobbing. Bull's eye, preacher man.

14

LUCK

HAVE OFTEN described myself as lucky—lucky to have been born where I was, in good health, good circumstances, and, above all, to Bill and Joan Burgess. But there's something insincere, something disingenuous about that sentiment. An element of pride shows through. Yes, I'm lucky—lucky to be the thoroughly splendid fellow I am today, and talented to boot. Of course I owe some credit to my wonderful parents. Bet they feel lucky too.

If I truly acknowledge the depth and quality of my luck it leaves no room for pride. Luck laughs at pride. So much of what we accomplish depends on the advantages handed us. As Texas politician Jim Hightower said of the first President Bush: "He was born on third base and thought he hit a triple."

Luck is one of life's guilty secrets. Everyone prays for it. But few credit its true impact.

I could have been born a meal rat, bred to be fed to captive snakes. I could have been born before the invention of dental anesthetic. I could have been born on La Chureca, the massive Managuan garbage dump that is home to a couple of hundred families. I could have been born to a teenager in a neighbourhood where the closest thing to industry is liquor stores and 7-Elevens, and social clubs revolve around red and blue and shooting at rivals from cars, places where luck can mean surviving long enough to end up in the Darwinian society of prison. I could be born seemingly normal but without the simple common sense of a squirrel. Then the wheel might turn again and catapult me to fame as an O.J. Simpson juror. There's no telling about luck.

Writers from Jared Diamond (*Guns, Germs, and Steel*) to Malcolm Gladwell (*Outliers*) have mused on the effects of chance on the history of nations and people. Social anthropologists like Diamond make the point that the structure of our civilizations often depends on factors—arable land, climate, types of fauna, etc.—not of our choosing. Like the chances of joining an exclusive fraternity your opportunities tend to depend on where you're born.

Calvinists don't believe in luck. They call it predestination. Calvinists, among others, believe God decides whether you will be saved or damned before you are even born. Then, having chosen your fate, He damns you anyway—rather like breeding a legless dog and then beating it for not fetching sticks. (It would be a handy system if we all got notified of our status via registered mail, or perhaps colour-coded birthmarks. A pre-damned individual could save a lot of effort regarding hygiene, loan repayments, and such.)

I consider it a piece of luck that our preacher Daddy was no fundamentalist. Dad never bought into the restrictive message of John 14:6: *"I am the way, the truth, and the life: no man cometh unto the Father, but by me."*

Dad knew this model was far too random. If Jesus really is the only path to salvation, how could salvation be so dependent on chance? For thoughtful Christian believers, it represents a nasty little philosophical problem. Will a baby born in Delhi, steeped in the Hindu faith of his fathers, live a full, rich life, and go to his reward—eternal damnation, because he lacked the good fortune to be born in Dallas and raised a Baptist? Mr. J. Calvin had no problem with it. Others find that idea rather perverse. But then, no one ever said life was fair. Why should the afterlife be different?

Not for nothing did the Greeks personify the Three Fates who decide the course of our lives. Because, as we experience it, chance can seem indistinguishable from the will of an unseen force. The Old Testament story of Job, a good man afflicted by God with one calamity after another, has a contradictory sort of reassurance to it. The fact that God is doing it all on purpose at least suggests that noble Job is not simply experiencing an epic run of bad luck. That would make the story even more frightening. When it's God you can always try sacrificing a goat. When it's pure bum luck there's not a thing you can do.

My siblings and I always understood that we had been fortunate. Throughout our lives, we experienced moments of revelatory comparison. We loved our mom and dad. But it was when we caught glimpses of other worlds that we understood our luck. My trip to the coast with Al's family was a dramatic example, but there were other small reminders from time to time.

Once when I was eighteen or so, a girl I knew came to the house to give me a ride to a party. Dad wandered into the dining room, said hello, and we chatted a bit before saying goodbye. On the way to the car my friend asked, "Was your dad drunk?"

Definitely not, I assured her. "So he's always like that?" she marvelled. "He seems so happy."

Some parents are cold and stern. Some can be manipulative and emotionally cruel. My friend Laura is the kind of intelligent, multi-talented, gorgeous woman that any sane parent would prattle on about until the neighbours feign choking fits just to change the subject. But while still in her twenties she lost her mother to a drunk driver. And every year thereafter, Laura's father would write a birthday letter to his late wife. In this annual message—reliably distributed to Laura and her sister—their father would describe to his departed spouse all of the ways that his daughters had disappointed him in the past year. Wherever she was, Mother was no doubt expected to be deeply disappointed as well.

Parents, health, circumstances—that's macro-luck, the kind that helps to shape our destinies before we take our first steps, placing us up the track with a nice head start. Macro-luck is the most easily overlooked variety. Luck, as most of us recognize it, is the day-to-day run of circumstance, the random chance that falls one way or the other.

Yet even here, true luck can be hard to recognize.

Back on that Brandon construction site, when my young face was impaled like a chicken kebab, I wasn't thinking, "Score!" even though the placement of that rebar was almost surgically fortunate. Just because I had a metal rod sticking out of my head doesn't mean I wasn't lucky. Later when the drinking started I became incontinent while passed out, regularly waking up soaked in urine—another lucky development that motivated me to sober up. The breaks I've had, it's a wonder friends don't resent me.

However, nobody likes a Pollyanna. People who try to look at the bright side of every parking ticket are in denial, and also annoying. My mother has Parkinson's.

There's no good side to that one. When bad luck arrives you can only hope the damage will be limited—perhaps some pain, some inconvenience, and a good story to tell afterward. Maybe even some flattering weight loss, as when, in the summer of 2003, Fate touched my digestive system.

The cozy corner restaurant on Paris's Rue Monge featured a sign with the familiar laughing/crying theatrical masks of Comedy and Tragedy. Fate was giving me a heads up. Failing to take heed, I ordered the seafood spaghetti. Tragedy struck roughly twenty-four hours later. I was in room 13 of Hotel Esmeralda across from Notre Dame Cathedral when it hit with fever and shakes, my jaw chattering like that of a hunting cat, eventually settling into a three-day subscription to the Bacterial Slim-Fast program. The housekeeper would peek in, see me on the bed and flee before I could speak. On day three I got it out: *"Je suis malade!"* Soon a sympathetic desk clerk was leading me across the Seine to Hôtel-Dieu, the old hospital beside the great cathedral.

Blood tests revealed nothing serious—just another gut-twisting episode of *Catch-of-the-Day Strikes Back*. Maybe the mussels, or the shrimp, or the main suspect, a raw oyster balanced neatly atop the plate. "Not even in season," the doctor sniffed.

"Pourquoi," I moaned, "did I order seafood?"

The doctor shrugged. *"C'est le destin,"* she said. Fate.

Next day I sat in a café on Boulevard Saint-Germain, shaky, fifteen pounds lighter, and almost tipsy with gratitude for my return to the world. I had planned carefully for that trip—part vacation, part travel-writing excursion. But what had I been planning for? Buying the tickets, laying out the itinerary, never realizing that in so doing I was making meticulous plans to place myself in a Paris hospital with a tube emptying into my arm. That this had not been my intent was irrelevant. The doctor had been right, and so was Doris Day. Wherever you go, *que sera sera*. Fate is real. Read Robbie Burns a hundred times and you will still be unprepared when the plough turns up your nest and you truly understand what becomes of the best-laid plans of mice and men.

Travel plans in particular are a kind of hubris. We have erased the old difficulties that stood in the way of globe-hopping, and we pretend that it's all a simple matter of picking a spot on the map and then choosing your chariot. But the Fates are insulted. They send their silent seafood emissaries on ahead; they lie in wait for tourists, young athletes, oblivious pedestrians, and proud engineers alike.

Only months earlier the Space Shuttle *Columbia* had disintegrated high above Texas. Some of the world's finest scientists and engineers had collaborated to make such flights possible; billions had been spent to create the conditions that would allow seven astronauts to lose their lives in a maelstrom of shattered metal out at the edges of space. Not the plan, of course. But only on that day, February 1, 2003, the Fates revealed the end result of all that work and expenditure. Perhaps that result was neither willful nor preordained, but random. Seen in review, it looks the same.

What is the power of fate? How much of our experience is hostage to chance? When I consider the factors that shape character—in particular, my mother's character—I think about Daniel and Leonard Fong.

I wrote about Daniel and Leonard in a December 2010 *Reader's Digest* article. They were born in East Los Angeles to Chinese-American parents who ran a thriving little store called the Golden State Market. For the Fong family, fate arrived July 5, 1980, in the person of one John Westley Hayes. When Hayes and two other men walked into Golden State Market, Susan Fong was working the till; her husband Leonard Sr. was behind the butcher counter, near where eight-year-old Daniel was playing. Susan's mother was also in the store. Hayes shot and killed both of Daniel's parents. Although young Daniel would not remember it at the time, his grandmother was also shot and seriously wounded. Later Daniel would be a courtroom witness, describing the murder of his mother and father.

Daniel and Leonard were whisked off to cold Toronto to live with an aunt and uncle who didn't really want them. "We were always told we were stupid," Leonard says. "We were told that our teachers thought we were stupid. If we were five minutes late for dinner, we didn't eat."

The boys were never given keys to the house. If they did not get home by 10 p.m. the door was locked. Both Daniel and Leonard in turn would be thrown out of the house before turning eighteen, finding temporary homes and surrogate families among their friends. They marvelled at how those other families operated "[The kids] had keys, their parents cooked, left them leftovers," Leonard says. "You just matched it up with your own life and thought, 'Something's not right.'"

Eventually their story would take a remarkable turn. A couple of years ago Leonard discovered the location of their parents' grave—he and Daniel had never known it—and travelled to Los Angeles to visit the cemetery. Next, Leonard decided to visit the family home on Eastern Avenue. Intending to ask permission to look around, he knocked on the door. From inside, a woman's voice said something in Chinese. Leonard held his palm down a couple of feet above the ground. "I used to live here," he said, "when I was four years old."

The door flew open, and there stood two weeping women. One was Leonard and Daniel's aunt, the other their maternal grandmother. It turned out Daniel and Leonard had been expected—for thirty years. By the time their maternal grandmother had emerged from hospital her two grandsons were gone to Canada and the dead parents' estate liquidated. But at the estate sale their grandfather had stepped in, purchasing the family home in East L.A. From that day on, the home was kept exactly as it had been—not so much a shrine as a destination. The grandparents were determined never to move. Someday, they knew, the boys would come looking. The house must look as it always had. The lost boys had to be able to recognize it.

As Leonard marvelled over the familiar sights—even the wallpaper was the same—the room suddenly filled with aunts and uncles. "It felt like the SWAT team coming in," Leonard says. "People coming in the front door, the back door, the side door. All of a sudden the room was full."

There was a reason. The family had gathered from around the country for the funeral of Daniel and Leonard's grandfather, held the day before. The man who kept faith for so many years had reunited his family with his death—just in time to accomplish his heart's desire.

Few personal histories I've heard have illustrated so clearly the two faces of fortune. But there was another aspect of their story that was equally striking to me. That was Daniel and Leonard themselves.

A self-employed graphic artist, Daniel is in every sense sober—industrious, even-keeled, wise. Leonard is a top New York–based fashion photographer whose work takes him around the world. Two young men who essentially raised themselves, they would stand as a source of pride to anyone who could claim credit for the parenting job.

Their horrible experiences did not slip away without effect. Daniel attributes certain personal traits—an essentially conservative nature, a tendency to go it alone—to his life experiences. Not to mention a shudder that goes through him when he hears the sound of helicopters overhead, a legacy of the police choppers that hovered in the skies of East L.A. on that horrible day in 1980.

Yet Fate could not destroy Daniel and Leonard Fong. There aren't many who would have such iron-clad alibis for flying off the rails, for becoming drunks or crack addicts. People would have shaken their heads and said, "With all they went through, what did you expect?"

No excuses necessary, thank you. Daniel and Leonard Fong are doing all right. And in their success lies the mystery of human destiny. Some are consumed by flames, while others are tempered.

As many historical arguments as there are for the importance of circumstance, there are as many confounding examples of individuals who seem to have grasped circumstance by the throat and kicked its sorry ass. The human condition is no simple cake recipe.

Frederick Douglass was born into slavery in Maryland, to a mother who died young and a father he never knew, and rose to become an author, statesman, and one of the greatest orators of his era. His contemporary, Abraham Lincoln, born to an illiterate father in a one-room cabin, proved to be a voracious reader who largely educated himself. Jeffrey Dahmer was born to good parents in Wisconsin, demonstrated an obsession with death at an early age, became an alcoholic in his teens, and eventually gained lasting infamy as a cannibalistic serial killer. His mother asked that her son's brain be studied for possible abnormalities. Parents always want to know why.

Good parents, good outcomes—a simple formula. But human cause-and-effect is not so clear cut, and it wasn't necessary for us to meet Daniel or Leonard or Abe Lincoln to realize it. We only had to consider our own grandmother.

How did our mother, with her grace, her discretion, her exquisite sensitivity, spring from a woman with the grace of a tuba and the sensitivity of a stuffed sturgeon?

Young Joan Slorance got some bad breaks. But her circumstances would not define her. If our grandmother was a scorching flame, our mother would come away as steel. Like the Fong brothers, she was proof personified that our destinies need not be dictated by circumstance.

"Character is fate," said Heraclitus. The Greek philosopher, born in the sixth century BCE, didn't believe in luck. A person's destiny, Heraclitus said, is determined by his own innate qualities. I think he meant the kind of fate that descended on Richard Nixon, whose essentially paranoid nature eventually created the enemies he imagined; he meant people like the Fong brothers, unbroken by a youth that reads like a modern-day Dickens novel; he meant people like my mother.

Character was fate for Joan Burgess. Her nature trumped her circumstances. Was my mother a little lucky as well? Sometimes. The wobbling roll of a football, the chance to meet a young man who would balance her natural introversion and self-doubt with sunny optimism and a steady shower of adoration—good luck, certainly. Eventually she would have the good fortune to be survived by her children, though on occasion it would be a close-run thing. And in the final phase of their lives she and her husband would have chance to enjoy the fruits of their relationship. Whether that is really luck or the reward for hard work and perseverance is debatable. It was justice, at any rate.

Mom would retire from teaching in 1989. Dad retired a year later. They began taking long walks together each morning, and on these walks their plans took shape. They would embark on their more strenuous dreams first, while still physically able. And they wasted little time, embarking on a tour of Europe in 1990, donning straw hats in Venice and posing in them in front of landmarks from Vienna to London. They attended educational "elder hostels" around the world. They made regular tours of the kids—east to Toronto and Mississauga to visit Lynn's and Jock's families, and off to the West Coast to see Leslie's family in Whistler and my bachelor digs in Vancouver, with visits to their favourite beachfront cabins in Lincoln City, Oregon, squeezed in on the way down to visit Joe and family in California. There were family reunions, church activities, community causes, good friends.

In the late summer of 2006 they came west. These later visits to my West End Vancouver apartment held a special savour for all concerned. Mom and Dad would stay a block down the street at the Buchan Hotel, a quaint old pile notable for a mention in an Alice Munro story. We'd go walking in Stanley Park, then order in pizza and watch Toronto Blue Jays games at my place, free from any obligation but enjoying each other's company.

By this time I had—belatedly—reached the adult stage where one's lifestyle and apartment no longer inspire discrete parental cringes and despairing sighs. I had learned to vacuum. Clothes did not sprawl over furniture like badly trained pets. My beloved black cat had died years before, never to be replaced in my heart, never to fill another litter box with aromatic biscuits. (Once, when I was living in a previous apartment, Mom and Dad had bought me a vacuum cleaner and Mom had immediately put it use on the accumulated cat hair. "My God!" she said after the first pass. "This carpet is pink!")

My new one-bedroom place was furnished with pieces I had found and shipped from Asia and Morocco. It looked good. And I knew that every time my mother saw my circumstances she silently revisited the era when stacked crates of empty bottles perfumed a succession of

squalid basement suites, mute testimony to my dangerous priorities. I knew that just sitting in my clean and
well-furnished apartment gave her quiet satisfaction. On
some level, that may even have been the whole point of
having one.

One evening as we sat at my dining room table Mom
talked about the retirement years they'd spent—by that
time almost seventeen years, most spent in good health
and braced up by mutual love and support, their struggles
behind them. "That time was probably the best of our
marriage," Dad would later tell me.

As my mother turned toward me that evening at my
little table, I was surprised to see her eyes were wet. Her
tears may have represented simple nostalgia. They may
also have been a sign of inner knowledge. As we sat there
enjoying each other's company, my mother already sensed
that irreversible changes were underway.

But dark forebodings were not her subject that evening. Her subject was gratitude, and her eyes were shining. "I know we've been lucky," she told me.

15

A NIGHT IN THE LIFE

ABOUT THE only good thing you can say about a fiftieth birthday is that it beats the alternative. Fiftieth birthdays are best spent in the company of people you don't have to, and in fact could not possibly, lie to about your age—people who are well aware of that round number that has suddenly attached itself to your personal biography like a fat, loathsome tick. You want relatives for this party.

It was a good fiftieth birthday party, as far as it is in my experience to say. We celebrated at the Clear Lake cottage where we had passed happy summers. Our old friend Dianne Cooper had lent it to us for a week. My birthdays always were a little bittersweet, coming as they did in the last week of August, providing a final benediction for summer vacations almost complete. My birthday was traditionally a time for corn-on-the-cob, and now that I was all grown up there was no longer the horrible possibility that some well-meaning fool would make me a birthday present of new school supplies. Someone did, however, insert a big plastic spider into some gift wrap. I screamed and jumped and everybody howled. Like old times.

On this night the nostalgia was a little too much for Dad—he was uncharacteristically blue. Mom had been unable to join us. The difficulties involved in bringing her along on the seventy-mile drive, bringing the necessary gear for her tube feedings and medication, laying out contingency plans for any emergencies, had led her to fits of anxiety. When I assured her that everyone would understand if she didn't make the trip there was relief, but guilt too. "I'm sorry," she whispered.

There was another problem. We had a nursing shortage. Mom's needs were outdistancing available resources.

In our determination to keep Mom at home, we relied heavily on the professional services offered by our neighbour Donna Hamm through her private company, Caring Companions, and for the rest relied on nurses from the provincial government's Home Care program. Everyone had been performing heroically, but this month there were problems. Home Care's services were overtaxed, and Donna's people were not licensed to provide overnight nursing care. If we wanted to enjoy a family holiday at Clear Lake, each of us would have to take overnight shifts watching Mom. My shift, it just so happened, began late on the evening of my fiftieth birthday party.

Around 9 p.m. I offered my thanks, cursed those responsible for the plastic spider, said my goodbyes, and left for Brandon. I had the dark, unlit highway almost to myself, battling the vicious crosswinds of an incoming summer storm. I tried not to be anxious. But I was afraid.

They look after us when we are children. We repay the favour when they're old. That's the simple, circular formula celebrated in touching fable and humorous greeting card. But this is not the Old Country, and the scales are rarely that balanced. Those of us lucky enough to be shepherded through our foolish youth by good parents are hardly ever forced to pay our bill in full. Infirmity is usually, mercifully, brief. Modern families have access to resources that ease the burden, often completely. Nursing our elderly parents is not a given anymore.

As Mom's health declined we were determined to keep her at home. She dreaded the hospital and gained strength from familiar surroundings. Even as her precious ability to control her own environment slipped away she maintained what control she could. It could be inspiring, as when out of nowhere she would suddenly remind Dad of some obligation or appointment he might have forgotten—still running the household even as she struggled with basic functioning. But her independence also meant getting out of bed for no discernible reason, intent on tackling some task she could not articulate. We lived in dread of the serious nighttime fall. A baby monitor sat beside her bed, as well as a bell she was to ring to wake Dad if she needed help. In fits of anxiety she might ring for reasons she could not explain when help arrived. There were times when dreams and reality would blur for her, and in her terror the bell would ring. This was Dad's life most days. On occasion it fell to the rest of us. Tonight, my turn.

The fear and anxiety raised by the prospect seemed a shameful little secret. How could a son begrudge his mother the care that is her due? I comforted myself with the thought that the discomfort was surely mutual. Already we had shared a rite of passage we had surely both dreaded. There had been an afternoon, between nursing shifts, when I had taken Mom to the bathroom for more than a simple pee. Lynn and Leslie had done the job before, as had her husband. But I think she had wanted to spare herself and her sons the same indignity.

I sat her down, then helped her up and prepared to clean her with a wad of toilet paper. I was thinking it, but it was Mom who said it: "We've come full circle."

Helping me through, as always.

My mother, fiercely independent as a badger, would surely rather have seen any fate but this—gradually incapacitated, her ability to communicate decimated, yet not granted the mercy of oblivion. Unlike her own mother Mom was not spending her final days running for Prime Minister. Inside her deteriorating shell she was still present, still fighting to punch through, still sufficiently aware to understand how far she had fallen.

The wind was blowing hard when I arrived at Riverheights. The evening tube feeding was long over and Gaylene, her favourite nurse from Caring Companions, had put Mom to bed. It required both skill and finesse. Mom's body was gradually stiffening, petrifying. To move her into bed you first sat her down carefully on the edge, then lifted her legs and swivelled her into a prone position. The toughest part was turning her on her side, as she preferred. The first time I tried to wrestle her over she got panicky and called for Dad. I then discovered that the real experts—Dad, the nurses—had a trick. First they laid a short quilted sheet down on the bed. Once she was placed on it, they gave it a sharp tug and flipped her on her side. It was a little like pulling a tablecloth off a loaded table, except that in this case you wanted to accomplish a half-turn.

Not so long ago Mom might still have been up, watching TV. But she watched less now. Media input had become difficult for her to process—too much, too fast. Even her beloved Toronto Blue Jays had slipped from her list of priorities. She could no longer spare the horsepower required to pay attention. It now required all her focus and energy just to maintain a basic level of operation.

Some months earlier I had landed a short guest-hosting slot on a CBC Radio program. Mom enjoyed the opportunities such gigs presented. Unlike her husband she did not knock on neighbours' doors to inform them of the air time and dial position. But nonetheless she loved to listen. This time Dad took the radio into her room so she could hear the show. She asked him to take it out. The sound from the small speaker, the theme music, the competing voices in discussion—too much. The one-time pleasure of listening to her son on national radio was now just so much signal noise.

Tonight the apartment shook with groaning, whining sound. Dad's big bedroom occupied the top southwest corner of the building, with a bay window jutting south to intercept the wind. When storms blew in from the wide, empty fields that stretched west the bedroom creaked and rattled like the cabin of an old sailing ship. I lay in Dad's bed, straining to hear the sound of a bell above the din. It seemed impossible that one could sleep in such circumstances. It didn't even seem advisable.

I did, though. When it finally came the ringing of the bell drifted in to my consciousness as though from a wind-tossed ship. How long had it been ringing? I launched out of bed and across the apartment, calling as I went: "Here I am, Mom! I'm here."

There was panic in her voice. "I rang. But you didn't come!"

"I'm sorry, Mom. Can I help you up?"

She turned to me, and her eyes seemed to focus. "Steve," she said weakly. "Why are you here?"

She was awake now, her native solicitousness returning as the panic ebbed. "How was your party? You had to come back. That's not fair."

Almost commensurate with her aversion to attention was her desire to be no trouble. Once when my parents and I were staying in a hotel Mom had gotten up in the night, tripped over the bed cover on the way to the bathroom, and fallen hard. Next day she couldn't move her wrist. Yet she refused to visit a clinic lest it disturb plans Dad and I had for the day. It became necessary to get tough. No one was leaving the hotel room, we assured her, unless it was to visit a clinic. She finally caved. It turned out to be a serious sprain.

There were different rules for different relationships. Her children were her responsibility. There were no price tags, no conditions—she would never demand the payment due. With Dad it was a little different. Fifty-seven years of intimacy meant both trust and obligation. If she was to retain her tenuous grasp on liberty, his help would be required. She had to be tougher with him.

His intentions were the best. But he was not exactly a natural empath, and his approach to Mom's well-being generally involved calories. One day Mom was feeling nauseous after a tube feeding, something that happened when her stomach filled too quickly. The nurse suggested she lie down. Dad suggested food. "I have a nice half of a sandwich here," he said brightly.

Mom looked at the nurse with a grim smile. "He just doesn't get it," she said.

As Mom's condition worsened, some of the kids showed flashes of resentment toward Dad. While we watched a football game one night Mom rang her bell. She had become twisted in her bedsheets and was struggling in distress. Lynn and I bustled about, straightening, smoothing, soothing as best we could. "You're missing some great plays," Dad called out from the living room.

And yet the impression left by such moments was misleading. Dad wasn't callous—just sometimes clueless. His habitual demeanour had always leaned toward the cheerfully oblivious. It explained why the marriage relationship had been punctuated by interventions, with Mom periodically grabbing him by the lapels and letting him know that action was required on some behavioural issue. Once brought up short, Dad was always willing to adjust.

The adjustments were harder these days. Dad was in his eighties. His heart was a leaky boiler and, lest we had forgotten, a diagnosis of Alzheimer's had been made several years earlier.

Dad had never accepted that diagnosis. As years passed, neither did I. There had been some strange and terrifying moments. After a 2006 trip to the West Coast to visit my sister Leslie and I, Mom and Dad had returned to Brandon and dropped their suitcases in the bedroom. Next day Dad saw the bags and asked, "Are we going somewhere?" Reminded of the trip he could not at first recall it, even though he clearly remembered things that we'd done out west.

He insisted it was an isolated incident brought on by a moment of fatigue. But we were terrified, bracing ourselves for the horrors to come.

They didn't, really. Dad's short-term memory continued to be appalling. But his personality remained unchanged, his practical abilities unimpaired. Besides, Dr. Molecule was convinced Dad had Alzheimer's, and in our family that was considered solid evidence to the contrary. "He doesn't have enough of the symptoms," I once argued to Molecule.

"Well," Molecule replied, "it's still in the early stage." Five years after the initial diagnosis.

Our bad luck in the doctorial lottery had forced us into a more skeptical view of medical opinion. We had become warriors for proper diagnosis and appropriate attention. There was a price to pay for this. As much as we disliked Dr. Molecule it was clear he did not warm to the sight of

Burgesses coming down the corridor, either. Still, risking the animosity of our family doctor seemed an unavoidable option. We couldn't afford to relax and let things be.

We were concerned about Dad for another reason—he was in charge of Mom. Dad needed plenty of reminders to keep track of his own complex regimen of prescription drugs. He frequently messed it up. Yet he was the last line of defence for our increasingly disabled mother as well, the one who was there when the nurses went home.

It was not ideal. But my stormy night spent lying in his bed, wanting sleep yet fearful of missing the bell, had been very educational. My father, eighty-three years old with failing eyesight and an increasingly unreliable neural network, was fighting this battle every day and night. And doing a pretty fine job.

In the morning I got Mom up and into her chair as we waited for the morning nurse to arrive. I disappeared into Dad's bedroom looking for something to wear, finding one of his pajama tops. I threw it on and went back out to sit and chat.

Mom looked at me with the implacable gaze that was now hers by default. "I am feeling anxious," she finally said, "because I can't remember your name."

"I'm Steve, Mom," I said as casually as I could, moving over to crouch by her chair. "Your son, Steve."

"You're not Steve," she said. "Steve is the youngest. If you're Steve, what does Steve do?"

"I'm a writer, Mom."

She seemed to contemplate that for a moment. "Steve is a writer," she said finally. "You're wearing Dad's pajamas."

Apparently that had been my mistake. The pajamas had thrown her. I crouched beside her, feeling the same sort of tingling shock as on that Christmas Eve when I had found her lying on the kitchen floor, blinking at the ceiling.

There was a knock on the door, and the morning nurse entered. She eyed me as she mixed up the meds on the dining room table. "You look like you could use a break," she said. "Do you need to take a walk?"

I did.

To be forgotten by my own mother was a rabbit punch. But to forget your own son was surely worse. And it was a particular cruelty of Mom's condition that it did not leave a healing balm of forgetfulness in its wake. When the temporary cloud of confusion lifted, Mom remembered everything that had occurred. That evening as I put her to bed she was crying. "I forgot my own son," she whimpered.

16

RIVERHEIGHTS
TERRACE

F OR THE handful of Second World War
veterans among its residents, Riverhe-
ights Terrace must bring back memories. You never know
when the guy next to you is going to buy the farm. Don't
get friendly with the new recruits. Best to stay detached.

Located on the western outskirts of Brandon, Riverheights Terrace is not what we used to call an old folk's
home. It is called, officially, a "holiday retirement community," although just when Brandon became a holiday
destination is hard to say. There's no nursing provided.
Seniors rent the serviced apartments and suites, all with
big TVs and no stoves. The motorized chairs gliding
silently along the hallways can create the feel of a *Doctor
Who* episode. Three times a day moto-chairs and walkers converge on the huge central dining hall. Better not
leave it too late—residents start rolling in an hour early
to grab choice seats. After mealtimes the walkers jam up
at the single elevator like Manhattan taxis at rush hour.

The rest of the time there's bingo, whist, carpet bowling, singalongs, movie nights, and the occasional bus outing.

Turnover rates are high—the sales force can never rest easy. When residents periodically disappear from view it's as likely they're in Brandon General as on vacation. Some don't come back. It seems that almost every second week the big noon meal is preceded by the announcement of a memorial service. It's not all gloom though—they're singing "Happy Birthday" to somebody every second day. Stay a while in Riverheights Terrace and you get to be as sick of that tune as a Chuck E. Cheese waitress.

You might expect a place like Riverheights to be full of ghosts. Certainly there's a palpable sense of absence as nameplates suddenly disappear from doors and habitual dining table quartets are forced to fill new vacancies. But ghosts? Spirits hovering over the rows of tables, roaming the long carpeted hallways lined with flowery prints, past rows of doorways and parked walkers? Not likely. Ghosts are about passion and unfulfilled desire. Here all feels played out, denatured. Any tormented souls currently paying rent at Riverheights will do their future haunting elsewhere, in the houses and fields and high schools where their unresolved torments were born.

Not that Riverheights lacks tension. There aren't enough hormones to truly make it like high school. But with a sedentary population commuting back and forth to the dining area and activity room, Riverheights is in effect a self-contained small town. The social dynamic is lively and the gossip unavoidable. While it's hardly a soap opera (unless you're thinking *General Hospital*), there are characters in residence. And hidden behind Prairie stoicism, there is real pain. The residents in this place generally arrive two by two and leave one at a time. Someone gets left behind.

One evening while heading back to my parents' third floor apartment I see a shirtless old man lurch into the laundry room where an elderly lady is busy folding her clothes. "Are you as lonely as I am?" he asks her without preamble. "It's been two years since my wife passed. I'm so terribly lonely. But I knew she had to go, you know, she was in so much pain. She had leukemia you know, blisters all over her body. She couldn't even roll over. I couldn't do anything for her… couldn't do anything for her…"

I freeze in the hall, horrified—sympathetic for the man but frankly more sympathetic for the poor, quiet woman folding her laundry. After all, by his own admission he's been a widower two years. If this is still his conversational opener without so much as a how-do-you-do, I would guess he usually dines alone.

"That's old Nick," Dad tells me later. "He drinks quite a bit. Most of the ladies here are scared of him."

Understandably. Yet Nick's soliloquy is suggestive of more than just social discomfort. Could this be the emotional reality of life here? Could this be the soul of Riverheights laid bare?

I now recall that I have in fact seen Nick before, sitting with his door open at midday, shirtless, listening to sentimental old melodies. He appears to be an anomaly, the only obvious drunk in the place. But who knows how many grieving Riverheighters would make similar confessions but for sobriety and self-control? Particularly among the widowers—men of that generation are usually said to have a harder time after the death of spouse. For elderly women it can be a secret relief no longer having an old man to care for. If healthy, older women tend to be far more self-reliant. Men are more likely to be lost, a fate the family has long feared for Dad. *In vino veritas*—I wonder if, deep in his cups, Nick may speak for more residents than they would admit.

Not that it's all elderly widows and widowers in Riverheights. There are at least a couple of young mysteries here. Alan is a short, boyish looking guy who likes to stay up late in the TV room watching Turner Classic Movies. He may be a little older than he looks but he can't be that old—mid-fifties at most. He's one of at least two younger renters here.

What brings a younger man into this world? The lack of need for a stove, certainly—plenty of bachelors would go for the three-squares-a-day aspect of Riverheights. Still there is something disconcerting about seeing a man place himself in this milieu decades ahead of schedule. The young stick out here. No visitor bounds up the open staircase that leads from the dining room without instantly feeling self-conscious—any visible display of strength or agility seems rude here. Young people are intruding. This is a small world with its own atmosphere, and it can be stifling. There's something of the hospital here, a place filled with uncomfortable reminders of the human condition, the kind of place that inspires in some people a near-phobic reaction.

Then there are the people who thrive in this environment. In the coffee room a large woman in a larger motorized chair reads obituaries to a friend. "Dorothy Atkinson; Rosalie Boux née Simon; Margaret Batchelor née Gustafson; Maria Estrela; know her? Know her? That's all today." This woman is the self-appointed monarch of Riverheights. They call her Queen Julia.

If you want information about the residents of Riverheights Terrace—their health, their comings and goings—Queen Julia is the one to see. How Queen Julia received her nickname is unclear. But as she is perpetually enthroned in a deluxe motorized chair unmatched by any in the complex, it was perhaps inevitable. Her age is hard to determine. Julia is a large woman, with enough facial hair to land a midway job. Queen Julia is served first at mealtimes. This is not because the staff recognizes her royal claim—it's because she makes sure she is first to hit the dining room so as to commandeer the first table. At this point it's debatable whether anyone would take it from her. There would only be hard feelings, and it's unlikely anyone else cares as much anyway.

Queen Julia is one of those character studies one makes out of necessity rather than affection. She displays an odd combination of curiosity about her neighbours and ignorance of the world at large. But what curiosity it is. Not a sparrow falls in her kingdom but Queen Julia knows of it.

One day I am sitting in the activity room reading the paper. Queen Julia is a couple of tables over, sitting with a tall, gaunt resident I don't recognize. But he seems to know me—almost, at least. "Is that Joe?" the man asks Julia.

"No," Julia tells him. "Joe is arriving next week with his wife. That's Steve. He's the youngest. It's his birthday today. He and Bill are going to Albert's Restaurant up on the North Hill for a birthday dinner."

I had only made up my mind about Albert's about half an hour before.

"We don't need a newspaper," one resident mutters to me. "We have Queen Julia."

Riverheights Terrace is a bit like a three-storey Stoughton, a simulacrum of the small-town prairie life Mom had found so wearing years earlier. As such it hardly seemed a good fit. But for the most part Riverheights would turn out to be a pleasant surprise.

Mom and Dad's balcony looked out toward nothing but acres of farmland and a broad stage for nightly sunsets. Dad fit in with the social scene right off. The social aspect would not prove to be much of an issue for Mom. The progress of Parkinson's soon locked her into a world even smaller than Riverheights.

Christmas 2008 did not come heralded with the usual pleasant anticipation. We'd made it through a bad year. The worst, really, though it didn't look likely to hold the title for long. Flying east that December I tried to imagine scenarios, game-plan the ways some of our traditions might survive the new realities.

Many know the melancholy of Christmas—the dissonance between public celebration and private reality, the memories that make jolly Christmas trappings seem like cruel mockery. In years past I had sometimes shuddered to consider what Christmas carols might mean to me once my beloved Christmas world had gone. This year, it seemed, might offer a preview. I had to assume that this would be my last flight to Christmas Town.

One thing was certain—this year's Christmas hoopla would consist of whatever I could arrange. Once upon a time the accumulation of wrapped boxes had just seemed to spread naturally as kudzu, claiming more and more living room acreage as Christmas Eve approached. Now it was mostly up to me. I shopped for others, checked off my own gift list, and made frivolous purchases just to get boxes under the tree. Even now, though, Mom was determined to play her usual part. Weeks earlier at the close of a visit from Lynn, Mom had gripped her arm. "Christmas," she whispered. "Dad."

"A gift, Mom?" Lynn asked.

"Yes," she said. "Housecoat. Blue."

"Her face just relaxed when I said I understood," Lynn told me. "She was lying there worrying about it."

Now the blue housecoat was in my suitcase, ready for wrapping. Bottles of Glenfiddich and Dalwhinnie were easily identifiable beneath the tree. Pajamas and comfortable velour lounge wear was accumulating courtesy of donations from all five kids. And I had a mission to run, down to a little trophy store on 10th Street.

Thirty-nine years earlier my grandfather's final Christmas had been made by the trophy our cousins got for him. "I dunno, Steve," Lynn said. "Seems a little corny."

It did. Our mother had never been one to collect cheesy little tchotchkes. But over the years we had all learned that Mom's surface reserve could be deceptive. Presented with unabashed expressions of her children's love, she could be overcome.

After a 1995 family reunion, we had surprised Mom and Dad with a giant print of a family portrait, inscribed with the words "We love you." Five years later on the occasion of their fiftieth year together, we arranged for a stone bench a few blocks from 54 Clement, inscribed with the phrase: "Mom and Dad—it's been 50 years. So sit."

Mom wept when she saw the portrait. And they both loved that bench. They visited it, cleaned trash around it, tended the decorative foliage. It was always instructive to see Mom react to gifts and expressions of affection. The undeniable, concrete evidence of our devotion overwhelmed any discomfort and brought her to tears.

I picked out a red-and-gold trophy. Bonus—the shop had little Highland dancer figurines. I'd been concerned about that—a little gold bowler would not have worked. A golfer would have been worse. I got one dancer for the top and a different one for the middle.

Preparations for Christmas Eve involved new complications. Mom's tube feedings were an issue. After the feed bag had dribbled its way through the tube, nurses mixed her evening medications into a big plastic syringe and injected them through the tube, followed by a flush. Problem: The medications included sleeping pills. Christmas Eve, the nurses would not be able to show up late to delay that knockout punch. If Mom was to be able to stay up for Christmas Eve I had to learn the procedure so as to do it myself later in the evening.

A nurse showed me how to crush the meds in a bowl and draw them up into the big syringe. We uncorked Mom's stomach tube and delivered the mix nice and slow, followed by a flush. Mom sat patiently while I learned the ropes. There was some spillage at first but I got the knack. "Good job," the nurse said.

I knew of no standard by which I could calibrate my reaction to this success. Such an unexpected honour. Administering medication through a tube into my mother's abdomen—nope, I'd never had opportunity to rehearse a reaction. As it turned out I was rather proud. And Mom seemed pleased. We were ready for Christmas Eve.

The tree was up. The days of real Scotch pine were long gone for us, but they're doing some fine things with artificial foliage these days. Mom's baked snack mix had fallen by the wayside—we didn't even have an oven anymore. No one really thought it was necessary to mix up the traditional punch. Frankly, with all the bottles and packets of medication around we couldn't afford the table space anyway. Santa candles were everywhere, though. And there was a remarkable number of packages crowding the tree. Early in the evening Donna and Kelly Hamm dropped by with their daughter Amanda and her miniature dachshund. Mom loved her a good dachshund. Gaylene, her favourite nurse, came around too.

About two-thirds of the packages were for Mom. She was getting enough pajamas and comfortable lounge wear to satisfy Hugh Hefner. Dad loved his blue housecoat and, as always, the expensive Scotch. In moments of honesty he would admit that years of pipe smoking had made it a struggle to differentiate the good stuff from Bell's, his bargain brand. But he loved trying. And however it tasted, it was expensive Scotch, and a token of love. Had we been so inclined we could have rustled up some old Glenlivet boxes and filled up discarded bottles with cooking sherry.

Playing Santa was a full-service job now—hand out the gifts and open them too. The tall, roughly wrapped box I finally placed on her lap seemed to inspire in her vague alarm. I peeled the wrapping and wrestled it out of the box—shedding red and gold glory, festooned with Highland dancers, and on its marble base the corny, heartfelt inscription: "World's Greatest Mom."

"Let me get a picture, Mom," I said.

She held onto it gamely, her face its now-standard mask of grim effort. "Smile, Mom," I coaxed.

Her face opened, as if in silent laughter. I clicked the shutter and froze that verdict on Christmas 2008.

Next day Gaylene stopped by to admire the trophy. "It was a close race," I assured her. "Mom was something of a dark horse candidate—split the vote and came up the middle."

Mom looked over at Gaylene, raised her eyebrows, and laughed. It might have been a scene from ten Christmases ago. Behind the frozen mask, between the temporary spells of confusion, our mother was still herself. Still there.

Mom rallied for evening battles. We even managed a movie night. I had brought along a copy of *The Red Balloon*. Made in 1956, it tells the tale of a boy and his pet balloon in Paris's Belleville district. Half an hour long and almost wordless, it was perfect for Mom's precious resources of energy and focus. In the magical finale our young hero is carried aloft by a cloud of bright balloons, without the aid of animation or a single computer. Mom was enchanted. And she made it all the way through.

There was a real Christmas dinner at our little dining room table, cleared of pill packs and draped with a new ten-dollar tablecloth. There was take-out soup from her favourite local diner so she could participate fully in the communion. Three days later she was once again helped into her black-and-red Christmas finery to sit down at the table and mark the 58th anniversary of that day when her lovely ankle-length wedding gown had confounded her fashion-challenged groom.

The three of us sat at the little table and toasted the occasion. Mom turned to me, speaking carefully. "And to you," she said, "for being so gracious...with everything..."

It had all proceeded miraculously well—a precious and unexpected gift, if not exactly like Christmases of yore. Had I been in a mood to reflect on the lessons of history it might have occurred to me to compare this holiday season of 2008 with another. It was in the Christmas season of 1944 that German troops surged forward from the Ardennes forest in a last-gasp attempt to drive Allied forces back to their boats. For a while there the holiday with Hitler was a pretty big noisemaker. But the Germans had been forced to expend most of their reserves of men and *materiel*. Afterward they were largely spent—most military historians argue that the Battle of the Bulge hastened the end for the Führer. And Christmas 2008 probably hastened the end for Mom. Reluctant as I am to compare my mother with the Nazi war machine, there are parallels there.

Now it was over. I was packing my bags for the two-hour shuttle into Winnipeg and then the three-hour flight west. Mom sat in her chair, slowly absorbing her liquid midday meal. Timing was always tricky—when the feeding was over it was straight to bed. I hoped to say my goodbyes first. But I was too slow. Before I could get organized the nurse was leading Mom back to her bedroom for post-prandial nap.

She was lying down by the time I entered the bedroom. "Mom," I said, bending over and placing a hand on her shoulder, "I have to go."

She looked up and managed a smile. Under different circumstances it might have been called a grimace—lips slightly apart, teeth visible. A bright intensity in her eyes left no doubt that she was bringing to both the effort and the moment as much focus as she possessed. She reached up and grasped me by the lapels. I stayed frozen there, bent over, not wanting to move yet unsure of how long I could maintain the posture. What I whispered I can't recall. Finally I pulled away, and turned to go.

It would not be our final meeting. But she would never see me again.

17

PARABLES OF JOAN

WHEN YOU'RE a preacher's kid you tend to see things Biblically. Even if you grow up to be a non-believer, you can't escape your influences, the drip-drip-drip of Sunday school into a malleable young brain. And as a non-believer, I don't wish to. With apologies to my Christian friends the riot and richness of Bible lore might even be better appreciated straight, without the addition of religious intoxicants.

The narrative stuff seems to travel best. Genesis is packed with wonder, horror, and perversion; Exodus is a screenplay. Cecil B. DeMille's epic *The Ten Commandments* still runs on ABC every Easter weekend and has surely had a greater impact on the North American public than its scriptural inspiration—DeMille was able to pare away the oddities of the Book of Exodus and get right to the crowd scenes and special effects. (If you're interested in the oddities, check out Exodus 4:18–31, the "Bridegroom of Blood" verses—among the most puzzling of Biblical head-shakers.)

Kings tells of heroism, power, and corruption; Job is a strange, magnificent outlier, a portrait of a bored and perverse God, toying with the human ant hill like a kid with a magnifying glass. Other books are neither narrative nor particularly edifying (if you want a rebuttal to all this wonder-and-magic-of-the-Bible stuff, try Leviticus. Much of it reads like a medical text written by post-apocalyptic hillbillies). Then there are the many non-narrative books of poetry, anguish, philosophy, and song—Ecclesiastes, the Song of Solomon, Psalms, Proverbs, and, in the Gospels, the parables of Jesus.

The instructive and often mystifying tales of Jesus are inextricably woven into Western popular culture and language. Thanks to Jesus the curse of a prodigal son became a blessing. There must have been plenty of bad Samaritans back in the day, but now, thanks to Jesus, no such thing.

The intended lessons are not always clear. Some of the apparently straightforward metaphors of Jesus can on closer examination become puzzling—the parable of the mustard seed has long been argued over, without any theological consensus emerging. But there's always a message in there somewhere. Every parable must have its point.

Good literature, however, should never be didactic. Somerset Maugham believed every well-told story of human behaviour would naturally prove instructive. No need for the author to slather some edifying moral on top, like wheat-grass icing on a birthday cake.

This book is neither popular fiction nor religious text. There's money to be made in both fields, but I lack the imagination for one and the paranoid zeal for the other. Whereas the Bible mixes history and legend, and literature seeks truth in fiction, this is the story of a woman and her family. It's a personal history reconstructed though memory, augmented by the minimum necessary amount of speculation. The goal is to describe a character, a strong and admirable soul whose influence lifted almost everyone she knew.

There's a credibility issue here. A man writing about his mother might be expected to embellish. Who's to say this chronicle is not just a variation on the golf career of Kim Jong Il?

Back in 1994 North Korean media reported that the Dear Leader had played golf for the first time, on a par-72 course in Pyongyang. According to the official news story, Kim Jong Il picked it up quickly. He scored five holes-in-one and shot 34 for 18 holes. That's a nifty 38 under par. His golf buddies must have owed Dear Leader free beers amounting to 40 percent of North Korean GDP. Quite a guy, that Kim Jong Il.

By contrast I can swear by the sacred couch of Oprah that my tale is true. And my case is helped by the modesty of my claims. My mother could not have scored a 34 in miniature golf. Nor was she a particularly marketable biographical subject—a reformed crack whore, or a folksy ex-governor. She was simply a woman who overcame and triumphed—a history exceptional in its way, but in most of its details thoroughly mundane.

So the tale of Joan Burgess is not too big a stretch. All the same, it cannot rest purely on personal opinion. Much better to rely on incident and, where possible, outside perspectives. When telling the story of a life, there ought to be parables.

Telling a loved one's tale often comes down to anecdotes, remembered and collected. Comprehensive histories, even of our most beloved, are not possible. As memoirists sometimes say, we are not born with tape recorders up our asses. We have to make do. If we don't remember every crucial moment and every precious conversation we search for meaning in the material we have.

And while secular histories must have narrative chapters, parables have their place as well.

Like DNA can be extracted from a strand of hair, character can be revealed by small events. So we tell the small stories we remember, sometimes mundane, and hope the details will reveal larger truths.

THIS FIRST Parable of Joan is not of the mundane variety. One summer Mom was commuting back and forth from our family cottage in Clear Lake, Manitoba, to her teaching job at the Assiniboine Community College. Dad was already on holidays and at the Lake full-time so Mom was joining in as best she could, making the seventy-five-mile drive back to Brandon every day. Out on the road one morning she saw they'd forgotten to fill the tank. She was worried—it was too early in the morning for most gas stations on this lonely highway. Halfway to Brandon at the town of Minnedosa she was relieved to see the Esso station had just opened, and pulled in. After paying the sleepy attendant, she came back out to the car and climbed in. Two men popped up in the back seat. "Drive, lady," one said. "Don't fuck around or we'll kill you and take the car."

Mom looked toward the station. The kid was nowhere in sight. She cursed herself for not chatting, perhaps getting an oil check or a windshield cleaning.

One of the men stretched out, throwing his legs over the passenger seat. The man sitting behind her draped his arm over her shoulder. The car reeked of exhaled booze. On their instructions she turned south on Highway 10, heading toward Brandon. In the early summer morning they had the road to themselves. On most such mornings it was a familiar and relaxing drive.

They were ex-cons—the prefix having been added very recently—and Natives from a nearby reserve. "Which reserve are you boys from?" Mom asked. She had taught enough Native students over the years to know something about the local map, enough to make chit-chat. She was intent on establishing a tone, steering the mood away from threatening or worse. She spoke calmly, asked simple questions, and slowly but steadily accelerated. The speed limit on the two-lane, gently winding highway was sixty mph. Mom brought the Volkswagen Rabbit up to seventy, then seventy-five mph. She'd never had a speeding ticket in her life. It was Mom's sincere hope that her first one would be written up any moment. Right about now would be good, thanks, officers.

Meanwhile her two passengers were bickering. It seemed there was a third musketeer, a buddy still behind bars. Porthos and Aramis were arguing about whether they should try to break him out, a project that might involve this vehicle in some yet-to-be-determined way. Or they might just go drinking. Their plans seemed a little unfocused. Mom let them argue as she searched the horizon for signs of the cavalry.

On weekends Highway 10 is full of young holiday makers, some in a little too much of a hurry to start relaxing. For that reason it is also frequently dotted with speed traps. But it was early, and a weekday. Police officers, fishermen, and grizzly bears all understand there is no point going down to the river if the salmon aren't running. Not a single cop was on the road; roadside billboards concealed nothing but tall grass.

The Trans-Canada Highway marks the northern city limit of Brandon. Thanks to Mom's expeditious driving it was approaching quickly. The call of that wide east-west thoroughfare seemed to have its effect on the two hijackers. They started to talk about the attractions of Winnipeg, the big city two hours' drive to the east—more bars, more pals, more opportunities for profitable misbehaviour. Apparently their incarcerated accomplice would have to wait for his big bust-out. The boys had decided to go east.

Throughout the drive Mom had worked cautiously to put a different spin on the circumstances, subtly establishing a different storyline. This was not a hijacking, but a lift willingly granted to two itinerant gentlemen seeking new prospects. Now that Brandon was in view it was only natural that she continue on to her job while they turned left to find their destinies. "I'm going to go on in to the school now, boys," she explained. "You should be able to find a ride to Winnipeg without much trouble."

Turning on to Highway 1, she pulled the car over. She held her breath as the two men piled out of the back seat. The door had barely clicked shut when she was spinning shoulder gravel, the little red Rabbit running as though from the shadow of a hawk.

Then she went to work and taught classes all day.

A DOMESTIC parable now.

When Joan was young and living in Bassano, her parents had taken in the orphaned Ada. It may have been one of the very few maternal examples Joan decided to follow. In the mid-seventies we gained two new siblings at 54 Clement.

Nancy was one of Leslie's best friends. A red-haired eccentric, Nancy was the kind of girl whose personal style might take her from small-town ridicule to a career in fashion or design; the kind of girl whose outsize personality and relentless truth-telling manage to be both exhilarating and scary, like a motorcycle with bad brakes. Nancy's equilibrium would soon be tested in the worst way. When she was about fifteen her mother died suddenly of a brain aneurysm. Within a year her father had been killed in a car accident. Suddenly Nancy was an orphan. So for the next two years she came to live with us. Many years later Nancy still found it hard to mention my mother's name without choking up—she told me she once burst into tears upon seeing some hotel sheets with the same pattern as the ones at our house. Some of those tears would be for her lost parents, certainly. But some of them, surely, were gratitude.

The other new arrival came to us through less tragic circumstances. Ron F. was Al C.'s old friend from those long-ago school days. I had since become buddies with both Ron and his older brother, Gord. They lived a few blocks away. Their mother, as I mentioned earlier, was a free spirit who had separated from her hockey-playing husband. We used to go over there a lot. Gord painted his bedroom black and covered the light fixtures with tinfoil. We listened to Deep Purple really loud. Mrs. F., upstairs with her boyfriend, didn't seem to mind. It was a very laissez-faire environment. Gord and Ron both had long delinquent histories—Ron had been one of our little break-in gang, and Gord would eventually do a three-month stretch in Brandon Jail for drug dealing. We smuggled him joints during visiting hours. (Shortly after his release the RCMP raided his apartment and found that hash pipe of mine. Happily, I never did time.)

One day Mrs. F. announced she was moving to Winnipeg, taking her two youngest children with her. Ron and Gord would stay in Brandon with their father. Very quickly that wasn't working out—Mr. F. wasn't interested in having the boys around the trailer. Nancy was already living with our family—I knew there was precedent. So I asked my parents if Ron and Gord could stay with us.

Mom and Dad sat down with Ron and Gord and laid out the rules. No late weeknights; no drugs or alcohol in the house; meals with the family; room and board to be paid by Mr. F.

Gord lasted about three weeks. I liked Gord—he was a carefree Philistine, a cheerfully amoral good-time Charlie. But he was apparently incapable of viewing authority figures, even well-meaning ones, with anything other than suspicion. Gord would skulk in the back door and disappear into the basement, rarely showing up for meals. My parents quickly grew tired of it, and Gord was asked to find other accommodations.

Ron was different. He showed up for meals. He referred to my parents as "Mr. Burgess" and "Mrs. Burgess." He never spoke about them to me with anything other than respect. Ron went to school, obeyed the rules. I was taken aback. He and I were still partying together at every chance—having a buddy as a housemate was great that way. But Ron was more careful than I was about keeping the house rules, for obvious reasons. And he liked it there. In hindsight Ron was getting traction on a different road. Eventually he would identify an affinity for math and calculation and begin a career at Revenue Canada. Not everyone's idea of a happy ending. But years earlier, hanging around in that room with the smoke and the black walls and the Deep Purple, it's about the last thing I would have expected. My mother cannot be given the credit for things that Ron accomplished on his own initiative. But seeing the way he reacted to my mother was a lesson, and a reminder, of what little miracles her influence and quiet example could achieve.

A POPULAR SUBSET of the Parables of Joan are the rescue tales. These were the occasions on which Mom's veritable Spidey sense for the emotional distress of loved ones led to decisive action or, in some cases, an almost Zen-like inaction.

"I was in Winnipeg for a week of training," Dad says. "As part of pastoral counselling we made a lot of hospital visits, and the training was intended to help us understand medical procedures. In the morning we watched an autopsy. Later that day we watched an operation from the gallery. It involved a spinal tap, with one of those huge needles inserted into the base of the spine. The surgeon pulled the needle out; I remember seeing the way the skin puckered up. Then I started to feel faint and I had to sit down."

Shortly afterward he called home, just to check in. Mom heard the tone of his voice, hung up the phone, jumped in the car, made the two-hour drive into Winnipeg, and took him home.

It wasn't the only time—she once jumped into a car and drove three hours to Fort Qu'Appelle, Saskatchewan, after hearing the weariness in his voice following a long and stressful encounter group.

As of the late seventies my parents were still attending and even running a lot of those. One memorable event was held in Winnipeg—both my parents attended. The group included a young participant in rough shape. His own mother had died after a long illness, during which his father had not behaved well, carrying on flagrantly with a girlfriend. Now the young man was filled with rage. That rage needed a target. Somehow that target became Dad. "I think you're a chicken shit," the young man snarled at him.

"Well," the group facilitator said brightly, "perhaps you need to work this out with a pillow fight."

"He would sort of wave the pillow at me," Dad says, "and then behind the pillow, he would punch me in the face."

The seventies were a stupid time.

Out-of-town participants were all sleeping in the same room, on mattresses. "In the middle of the night, Joan sneaked over to my mattress," Dad says, "to comfort me."

Fade to black. Faster, please.

The seventies, it is often said, were still the sixties for a stretch. Those of us too young to fully participate in the actual calendar sixties were intent on prolonging that decade till we could get our taste of it. Hitchhiking was part of that. The romantic call of the road was still drawing lines of kids out to Highway 1. My friends and I would all eventually join the queues, spending summer wages on Western adventures through the Rockies and on to the Okanagan Valley and Vancouver. But my brother Jock went first.

At Easter break of his grade ten year he convinced Mom and Dad that he could safely hitchhike to Regina to visit his childhood best friend. He had reached the town of Whitewood, roughly halfway, when darkness fell. There he stood as night closed in and all the helpful travellers apparently retired for the night. When a car full of fun-loving locals threw a beer bottle that narrowly missed his head, he decided it would be better to wait inside the Esso station café. "I spent the next miserable nine hours with a cup of coffee perched in front of me," Jock says. "The waitress kindly informed me about seven times that I would have to leave if I fell asleep, so I had to keep my wretched head propped up the whole time."

He had set out from Brandon a ramblin' man. But by 6 a.m. the spirit of wanderlust, so essential to the music of Woody Guthrie, had gone all squishy. Jock was rambled out. He made the walk of shame to the payphone and placed a collect call. "Mom answered the phone almost immediately," he says. "My next memory is of sitting out front and seeing the white Acadian turning in off the highway, with Mom's red hair visible behind the wheel. She had not a single word of reproach for me. She just seemed genuinely happy to see me."

MANY OF MOM'S character traits seemed to have been formed in opposition to those of her own mother. Grandma had been a viciously competitive bridge player; Mom could not be coaxed to sit at a card table. It was a breakthrough one Christmas when we played a few pleasant Scrabble games.

When it came to meddling, Grandma was a ninja. Coercion, pressure, emotional manipulation—that was parenting, pretty much. Thus Mom would sooner have her fingernails pulled out with hot tongs than stick her nose where it wasn't wanted. The "meddling mother" caricature so central to cartoons, domestic drama, and Jewish comedians' stand-up routines was, for us, just that—a stock image, like Snidely Whiplash. Our mother you had to beg to meddle.

"One of the things that was strongest for me was that Mom did not insert herself," Joe says. "In high school and after, there were periods where I was so depressed that I would sit there and listen to sad music. I dreaded leaving the house. She would just be with me, bringing me coffee.

"In my freshman year at University of Winnipeg, Mom and Dad would trek into Winnipeg to see me—Mom leading that charge, of course. Again, I was really depressed. We would sit there in a restaurant for an hour and I would say absolutely nothing. Dad would try to get me talking. Mom was quiet and would restrain Dad at times. But I also know that she was suffering right along with me."

Even when Mom knew that intervention was required, she possessed the subtlety of a Deng Xiaoping. There were occasions when, sensing something amiss with one of her children, she directed Dad to stay up late. "Don't ask about it," she would caution. "Just stay up and wait."

Mom knew the explanation would come easier in her absence. When it did she would slip out of bed to join the conversation and to prove once again that where she had received judgment her own children would be offered support, love, and wisdom.

That facility for empathy and understanding could show up at very unexpected moments. One afternoon when I was about twelve, Mom was sitting on the living room couch chatting with a friend, while I stood at the front door trying to get her attention. It wasn't working. Bursting with impatience and spurned entitlement, I pulled a handful of change from my pocket and flung it across the room to where they sat. The coins went *rat-a-tat-tat* off the living room wall, just missing the startled couch sitters. I braced myself. But Mom simply fixed me with a quizzical gaze. "You really need people to listen to you, don't you?" she asked.

It was not a rebuke. It was an observation, delivered as if by a film critic identifying a motif in a Bergman film. I stood there, ashamed and humbled. I can't remember what I had wanted to ask.

Parenting, like dodging bullets, is an existential activity. It happens in real time. Only in retrospect do you see the astounding variety of topics and situations a parent must handle. Even as I struggle to recall little bits of precious conversation my mother and I shared—gentle jokes, serious subjects—I am often reminded of the vast, random banquet of advice and information she was called upon to supply.

In grade nine I attended Rivers Collegiate, where Mom was teaching. "Steve," she told me one evening, "when I was standing beside you in the hall today I noticed that you need to start using antiperspirant."

Another puberty-related curve ball, and a deceptively tricky one. There are plenty of young men who get it wrong. Some opt for deodorant first, then shower; or shirt first, then deodorant; or most pernicious of all, deodorant, more deodorant, shirt, deodorant on shirt, and finally enough cologne to cater a hobo reunion.

Antiperspirant in hand, I had a question. "Mom— where are the sweat glands? On the hairy part of the armpit or below it?"

She thought a moment. "It's the hairy part, I think," she said.

Of course she was right. Whether in the realm of fact or opinion, Mom could be depended upon to steer her children right. One day when I was in grade three or four, I asked her to give me a bowl cut. What I really wanted was a Beatle cut, but I had misunderstood the terminology. Think of it—a harried mother of five, pressed for any break she can get, and here comes a sucker volunteering to be sheared like a sheep. Thirty seconds with scissors and a mixing bowl, and for once she might get a spare moment to flop on the living room couch with a cup of instant.

But no. "I don't think you really want a bowl cut, Steve," she explained.

I believe that incident alone marks my mother as a creature more elevated than ordinary humans.

Mom didn't share that assessment. In fact that kind of thinking could make her impatient. Someone singing her praises, as we kids often did later in life, would almost certainly annoy her. It's not that she considered herself a bad person. But she was painfully aware of her own shortcomings, and our lavish tributes rang false to her. I believe she found them dehumanizing.

Among the worst offenders was her brother Stan. He had a habit of composing hymns of praise that made his sister cringe. During one of his visits we were all at the dinner table, enjoying one of Stan's buffed and polished tales from his stock theatre days. Mom stood behind him, carrying a casserole dish hot from the oven. She wanted to put it on the table. The oven mitts were reaching the limits of their heat-shielding capacity. But Stan rolled on through his anecdote, unaware. Finally Mom got the dish down on the table. Stan reached out to help himself and recoiled. "Good Lord! That's hot!"

Delighted, he turned his gaze on Mom. "She stood there! Holding that scalding pot while I prattled on! She wouldn't say, 'Excuse me—hot pot coming through!' She just stood there burning up and waited..."

It was a good story. Our mother was indeed a stoic individual, as her brother gleefully pointed out. But Mom was pissed. Not just modest, or embarrassed by the attention—she was genuinely irked. "Stan," she said, "it was not like that."

Her reaction surprised me. What was it about Stan's reaction had upset her so?

"He likes to paint this picture of me," she said, "suffering quietly."

It was the suggestion of passivity, of resignation, that angered her. Joan Burgess would have you know she was no martyr. The woman who would survive medical malpractice and enough chronic conditions to kill a stable of horses was nothing if not tough. Respect, please.

18

END GAME

THE FLAT farmland west of Winnipeg is
still showing early March snow as I drive
toward the wide band of sunset. Leslie is in the passenger seat—the rental car is hers. I made a point of book-
ing the same flight as my sister. Seven months earlier on
this exact stretch of highway, a sleeping Greyhound bus
passenger had been decapitated by his deranged seatmate.
It's not as though I was really worried about how a fight
over the armrest might escalate in this part of the world.
I just didn't want to pass up the chance to catch a ride.

I'm speeding, in hopes of getting to the hospital before
they lock the doors for the night. Leslie and I spend the
drive in conversation, trying on and testing the various
options—hope, despair, fatalism, resignation. "Has Uncle
Stan called?" Leslie asks.

I am momentarily speechless. "Les," I say, "Stan died a
few days ago."

It's an honest oversight. I almost missed the news
myself, buried deep in one of Dad's emailed news updates.

Mom's older brother had been in failing health for a while and died after a brief hospitalization. Any other week it would have been a full-page headline in our family. As it was, our favourite uncle had been reduced to the status of a Bar-Kay. Four members of that excellent R&B outfit were killed December 10, 1967, in a Wisconsin plane crash. But the headlines were all about soul man Otis Redding. For our cousins, of course, their father played Otis—my mother, just a rhythm guitarist.

Here was a small silver lining, at least. Mom had slipped into a steady unconsciousness before news of her brother's death arrived.

Lynn had arrived in Brandon first, as usual. She and Dad take turns keeping vigil, not wanting to leave Mom alone for a moment.

Around the corner from Mom's room in the palliative care ward is a large common room for families and nurses. There's a kitchen and tables, a big screen TV, and budgies. One evening as Lynn is sipping coffee and watching the birds—one blue, one green, one white—hop and squawk in their corner cage, a nurse arrives to replace their feed. "Their names are Fiona, Shrek, and Patience," the nurse explains. "Actually, the blue one is new—Fiona the Second. The first Fiona got pecked to death. We got a ringer. Don't tell the patients. They have no idea."

The nurse sits down at Lynn's table. "I'm the one who called you. I thought you guys needed to know the situation. I knew your Mom. She taught me at Assiniboine Community College. Your mom was a role model for a lot of those young students. We always knew when she was coming down the hall—we could hear her shoes coming, click, click, click. She always wore lovely shoes. Such grace and dignity."

Leslie and I reach the hospital in time to get upstairs. Jock has already arrived in Brandon—Joe is scrambling to arrange his affairs in California. Lynn is in the hospital room when we walk in. She looks like forty miles of bad road. But I know there are worse sights coming.

Mom is on the bed, lying on her side in a blue-green hospital gown, eyes closed. Her white hair is a bright halo under the fluorescent light at the head of the bed. Her face seems changed. Then I notice her teeth are out. It makes quite a difference. Left at last with no more control over her own appearance, she looks more like her mother.

A plastic oxygen mask is strapped to her face. Lynn and Jock have been warning us to prepare for a shock. Not the sight of her, but the sound. Her breath is rasping like a rusty saw blade. Each intake of air shows its muscular effort, as though she were rhythmically lifting weights. It's too violent. It's not sustainable. And sometimes it gets even worse, louder and more erratic, causing panic episodes in whomever happens to be in the room. As bad as things have been from time to time over the past year or two, this is different. This looks like end game.

We have been told that Mom has double pneumonia—often the final, compassionate bullet that finishes a slow death. Not that we're all agreed about whether we've reached that point. Mom is still getting antibiotics, and Lynn, at least, is still armoured for battle. There is to be no surrender. Mom can still pull through.

Now that reinforcements have arrived it is time to organize deployment. I'm a night owl by nature—it makes sense that I should pull the overnight shift. There's a mattress and some bedding on the floor and a TV at the foot of Mom's bed. Our evenings are set.

I click through the programming guide, looking for something. Score, way up the dial in the sixties—*Robo-Cop*. I look over at the bed. "Let's give it another try, Mom. You'll like it better this time."

About twenty years earlier, in the waning days of the Reagan administration, I had dragged my parents to a Winnipeg theatre to see the new sci-fi epic from director Paul Verhoeven. "There's more to it than you think," I swore.

Later, over dinner, I was forced to apologize. Apparently the nuances had escaped them.

Now I am betting that, deep inside her oxygenated limbo, Mom is safely removed from the obnoxious intrusion of *RoboCop,* and prating nurses, and every other worldly annoyance. But is she? It's the water-cooler topic of the week.

Sometimes Mom's eyelids flicker—occasionally they drift open, though her eyes, when they briefly appear, do not move. What does it mean?

Nothing, I say. Lynn disagrees. Each flicker might be a response to some stimulus that has registered in her still-functioning brain. "See?" Lynn says. "I just said Dad's name, and her eyebrows moved."

False hope, I argue, a little Burgess family replay of the Terri Schiavo case. People in vegetative states are not usually inert. They move, open their eyes, make sounds, all signifying nothing more than the running of a headless chicken. Meaningless nerve storms.

Except when it means something. Medical history is full of stories of coma patients awakening, and even describing conversations held by their bedsides. Mom was a veteran of countless medical crises. Lynn and Jock had sat by her bed when she had not known them. She had swallowed her own wedding ring, yet returned to herself. Time and again she had beaten the doomsayers like Muhammad Ali rope-a-doping George Foreman. Vegas oddsmakers would be leery of betting against her at this point.

So I am playing along with Lynn's theory, just in case. Periodically I wind up Mom's old music box. It's a treasured heirloom that lulled us all to sleep as children, playing the three little melodies whose names we never knew, even as the notes were engraved on our little psyches like a Burgess subdivision of the collective unconscious.

I sing to her as well—standards like "Daybreak," which Mom once told me she bought on a Blue Jay seventy-eight, back in the thirties. But mostly I sing "Loch Lomond." That sentimental Scottish tune was played at her beloved father's funeral, piper and all. Years ago at a Robbie Burns dinner I had asked someone to teach me a few verses so I could do a little better than just parroting the "You take the high road and I'll take the low road" chorus. It's coming in handy now. I imagine Mom is impressed.

Or not. During one of my overnight vigils, I accidentally knock over a bedside vase. It bounces off the table, the wall, and the floor, clattering like a fire alarm. Mom doesn't even flinch. I keep singing to her anyway.

Sometimes Mom's breathing changes. This causes a flurry of activity, particularly from my two sisters. Everyone braces for the big moment. But there are plenty of false alarms.

One evening I am heading to the grocery store to buy provisions for a communal family meal at the hospital. My cell phone rings—it's Lynn. "You need to come now," she urges. "Mom sounds bad. If you don't start now you could be too late."

When I arrive, Mom is resting comfortably. I try to hide my impatience. Variations on the scene have played out several times.

My sisters hover over Mom, alert to every alteration. They tear up at every change in breathing. And me? Not so much. Watching their hair-trigger reactions, I am fighting annoyance.

But why? Our mother is dying. I know that. Maybe they're jumping the gun today. They'll be right soon enough.

I am embarrassed by my own moods, by my suppressed exasperation. Where does it come from? I suppose I just think there's no need to get worked up over and over again about the inevitable. Perhaps I am not ready to grieve. Once we get started, we might dissolve in a helpless mess. I want to function, to be strong for what's coming. Perhaps I am just trying to ignore the abyss and resent my sisters for staring into it.

Then again, perhaps I am grieving already. Who is the form on the hospital bed, mute but for her frightening breath? My sisters see their mother, a woman who is struggling, possibly in pain. Their tears express their love and empathy. I see a woman who is already gone, whose final quietus will be a formality. I am waiting. Perhaps my emotions are as well.

This is the flip side of first-time parenthood. There are no lessons—just the examples of friends who have been there first.

My friends Matthew and Laura had both suffered the untimely loss of their mothers by means respectively cruel and slow, and cruel and sudden. Early-onset Alzheimer's stripped Mrs. Mallon of her characteristic dignity and reserve, her faculties, her personality, and only then took her life. Laura's mother, still in her forties, taken away by a drunk—vibrant and alive one day, vanished the next, leaving Laura with only a helpless rage, paid off with a paltry jail term for the drunk.

Both my friends struggled with their loss. Months after the death of Laura's mom she dreamed they were walking together, talking, enjoying each other's company. "Mom," Laura asked, "Are you really dead?"

"Yes," her mother replied. "I am."

For the moment our mother is here. But a turning point has come. The medical team is suggesting that Mom's antibiotics be stopped.

A difficult call for anyone. And for us there's that added complication: the recommendation comes from Dr. Molecule. Our reflex reactions to his suggestions are almost hard-wired by now. Molecule says zig, Burgesses promptly zag.

But we have also been told that the drugs may be interfering with Mom's breathing. Even if she is breathing her last, we want that to be easier. And at this point it has become clear to all that the time has come. Let nature sweep all before it. The antibiotics are stopped.

Taking the night watch is more anxious now. I sit beside the bed, hold her hand, and pretend that the late night TV shows are a shared experience. Her breathing seems unchanged through the night. I turn in around 4 a.m., awakened mid-morning by Lynn and Les. Mom is still there, chugging away like a diesel generator. One tough customer.

There's a routine to my post-vigil mornings. A little breakfast at the hospital, then off to Forbidden Flavours Coffee and Ice Cream Shop for a double espresso, and at last a shower and shave back at Riverheights Terrace. Those espressos are heaven-sent.

At the café I am hailed by a high school acquaintance. I haven't seen Brian in decades. It tends to happen on these visits. "You're on the coast now, right?" Brian asks. "Lot of people out there. Ever run into D? He messed himself up pretty good. Wrecked that Corvette of his. Had to get new knees and a hip replacement too."

I hear my name again. The café manager is scanning the room, waving a cordless phone. "Is Steve Burgess here?"

I realize simultaneously that my cell phone is off, and that I am very predictable. I take the phone. It's Leslie. "Mom's gone," she says.

No one is crying when I walk into the hospital room, but their eyes suggest it's a temporary lull. Mom is lying with her face turned sideways. Her skin hangs down over her open jaw like a flat tire over a bicycle rim. Actors can't really play dead—you just can't make your muscles sag like that. It's not as though Mom looked great last night, and yet the difference is a shock. She's dead.

There's no holding it now, thank goodness. I sit beside the bed and cry. The end, they tell me, was quick. Jock had just left the room when Les ran to catch him. Mom's breathing was intermittent. Jock barely made it back into the room in time. Dad, meanwhile, had gone the other way. "He just stood up without a word," Lynn tells me, "as if there was something he'd forgotten in the next room, and headed straight out the door."

Moments later Lynn found him in the hallway. He looked at her like a lost little boy staring up at a cop. "Is she gone?" he asked.

There was nothing painful about it, as far as any observer could tell. She simply stopped. That indomitable little engine, that dogged pump with over eighty years of faithful service, has gone still. For the first time in her children's lives, we are divided from our mother by something more than mere physical space.

The next couple of hours are both vague and somehow vivid. A mist covers all of it now, some protective reflex of forgetfulness. Leslie says that she doesn't recall phoning me at the café. And although I remember the hours we spend sitting around that hospital room, talking, Mom still on the bed behind us, I can't remember a single specific topic. But there is laughter. We are telling family stories. Every once in a while I look over my shoulder at Mom, still on the bed, head turned, lifeless. Yet now, more than before, it feels somehow that we are there together. It feels like a gathering at the end of a long mountain hike—weariness, and yet with some sort of balm descending over all.

Reverend David Cathcart, minister at Knox United, drops by to pay his respects. "She was revered," he says simply.

It's quite a while before they arrive to take Mom away. I quickly wish I'd been absent. The nurses roll the body onto its back and now Mom's eyes and mouth fall open in a ghastly, vapid gape. It is no wonder we strive to separate body and soul in the face of death—if we did not, the sights we see might seem proof of lasting agony and torment.

That night we gather at a steakhouse. Dad has a little trouble with the remnants of his salad and starts eating it with his hands. We're all over him. This is the sort of necessary nagging that has been neglected over the past year or so. It's our responsibility now. The new era is beginning.

After dinner one carload heads back to Riverheights. But Dad decides to join me across the street at Forbidden Flavours for a coffee. He wants to talk.

The tables around us are full of laughing chatter as we sip our coffee. "I wasn't always a good husband to her," Dad says. "I was focused on my own needs. I didn't pay attention to what she was going through. I would come home and want to make love, but she would be at the end of a day battling with five kids and everything else.

"It was a very intense relationship right from the start. It was a very sexual relationship. She used to tell me, 'You're only interested in my body.'"

I have frozen myself into an attitude of receptive attention. I am wishing there was a mirror somewhere in my line of sight so I could check my face for signs of panic. Of course I must have understood all this stuff on some level. Five kids suggests at least some degree of familiarity and physical closeness. And I am touched and flattered to know that, in his most grievous hour, my father is opening his heart to me. But it's an unexpected honour. A guy ought to be given a warning that this kind of honour is about to be sprung. A deer on the highway should expect headlights too, but they almost never do. They just freeze and stare. And nod. I assume they nod, anyway. I did.

"You learned and did your best, Dad," I tell him. "You guys had the kind of relationship most couples never achieve. You had a wonderful retirement."

"We had a great time together. You know, in a lot of ways that phase was the best time of our whole relationship. We really became closer than ever."

"She told me how lucky she felt," I agree. Now I am getting the terrible feeling that the "happy retirement" and "sexual relationship" themes are about to merge. I brace myself. But to my selfish relief, the moment passes. We step back from the brink and sideways into fond remembrances, lingering to tell stories in the cheerful café.

Soon I must drive Dad home to Riverheights. He has spent many nights by himself in the two-bedroom apartment. And tonight there will be people there to keep him company. But tonight, for the first time, Dad is alone in the most profound sense. Many times in the past we adult children had played that morbid guessing game— who will go first, and who will be left behind? Most of us thought it would work out differently. Dad must have thought so too. It's unlikely he ever gave much thought to a night like this.

Whatever other purpose they serve, funeral services keep people busy. Relatives are flying in—nieces and nephews, and a couple of cousins I've never met—and people planning their contributions. Everyone is taking turns going through old photo books to choose snapshots for a big cardboard display. It's as self-defeating as trying to count salted peanuts. Particular photos lead to stories, expressions of admiration for particular phases of Mom's ever-evolving look, questions about bit players and extras. The goal is forgotten, restated, and lost again in some new reverie.

There's one last chance to see Mom. She's laid out at the funeral parlour, looking very natural. No heavy makeup. The morticians have done such a nice job that I begin to feel aggrieved on behalf of a profession that now seems to me unfairly maligned. As we leave it's a little shocking to recall that there will be no more sightings of this physical form. This was not a preparation for public viewing—it was just for us, perhaps to remove the memory of that last hospital image. Mom's next stop is not a casket.

The service is held at Knox United. The family enters the church as the attendees sing "Lord of the Dance." On the podium beside the pulpit stands a tall, plain wooden box holding Mom's ashes. There are two pictures—a recent portrait and the old 1945 picture Dad used to moon over during their separation. Beside the box is the Christmas trophy, adorned with the two Highland dancers. Say what you like, Moses, but there's a place for graven images.

Mom always wanted a pleasant sort of reception, a little wine-and-cheese affair. We hold it across the street at Brandon University. It goes well, a congenial celebration with some long-lost faces reappearing to shake hands and reminisce. Afterward we haul the flowers out to the car, some to keep, some to drop off at the homes of friends.

It's not enough, though. Too much like real life, like the hospital and Riverheights Terrace, where death is delivered like newspapers; not enough like Romeo and Juliet, where the entire audience is joined in weeping for the enormity of loss.

I suppose I never expected the heavens to open, the papers to call, banks to close, the mayor to announce a special day while fighting back tears. Still, we've got one more shot at it. Dad's a pretty popular guy.

19

TIME TRIALS

MOM HAS been gone for a couple of months. I have been travelling—France, northern Italy, and Rome. There is something humbling about Rome. The evidence of centuries, visible at every turn, produces an effect similar to that created by contemplation of the Milky Way. It puts you in your place.

Memento mori—remember you must die. That's the message of Rome. Usually the reminders come simply from contemplation of the generations that built and rebuilt the city. Sometimes the reminder is more direct. One evening I came upon a fatal accident on a quiet Roman corner—a seventeen-year-old girl, out on a Saturday night, had stepped off a curb and been hit by a scooter. She lay doubled over on the pavement, her dishevelled clothing revealing a lacy thong and perhaps a speculative plan for the evening. A bystander checked for a pulse and shouted: *"Un dottore!"* Minutes passed, and no ambulance came. Next day there was a bouquet on the corner with the inscription: *Una morta ingiusta.*

A little south of Circus Maximus, Death has carved out one of the city's most peaceful oases. It is marked by a pyramid. Not ancient by Egyptian standards, the pyramid does date back several decades before the birth of Jesus, a tomb for a prominent Roman named Caius Cestius. It backs into an enclosed yard split into two sections. This is the Cemetery for Non-Catholic Foreigners, sometimes called the Protestant Cemetery, most famous as the place where poets Keats and Shelley are buried.

The stone of young Keats is marked by one of history's most famous epitaphs: *This Grave contains all that was Mortal of a YOUNG ENGLISH POET, Who, on his Death Bed, in the Bitterness of his Heart, at the Malicious Power of his Enemies, Desired these Words to be engraven on his Tomb Stone: "Here lies One Whose Name was writ in Water." Feb 24th 1821.*

It reads like a young man's epitaph, a howl at the unfairness of early death. That is somewhat deceptive— Keats requested only that last, memorable line. The preamble was added by friends. It seems the greatest anguish was reserved for those left behind.

Keats's friend Shelley was so impressed by the Protestant Cemetery that he called it "The most beautiful and solemn I have ever beheld." He would be buried here in 1822, in the newer, more crowded, most beautiful portion of the cemetery. There are tight rows of monuments, flowering trees, and stray cats, all well cared for. In the midst of noisy, chaotic Rome, the peace of this stone garden seems almost supernatural. It belies the passion and complexity lying behind a simple stone, the hidden tales that make every cemetery a cousin of Spoon River. My mother loved the *Spoon River Anthology*, Edgar Lee Masters's collection of verses recounting life stories from a fictional town cemetery. And I know she would have loved this place, with all its implied mysteries.

A Canadian flag marks the grave of diplomat E. Herbert Norman. Why would Norman's grave be found here? A man whose career played out in Japan and Egypt, and whose purported suicide in Cairo has been a source of speculation ever since, was for some reason buried in this hallowed piece of Roman ground. Nearby, the 1899 tomb of Virginia officer Thomas Jefferson Page is decorated with fresh banners bearing the Confederate stars and bars. Other stones imply tragedy—children, teenagers, English youths who died while making the Grand Tour. Most were luckier, laid to rest in their beloved adopted city after long, distinguished lives.

Inscriptions on the older monuments are carefully worded. Prior to 1870, when Rome was ruled by the Vatican, it was forbidden to make any mention of God or salvation on these stones, lest anyone think that non-Catholics might be bound for Heaven. Many begin with the carefully worded formula: "Sacred to the memory of..." Beautiful as it is, the whole cemetery was intended to serve as a ghetto of the damned.

A beautiful cemetery can be a reassuring place. Elegant monuments offer evidence that lives matter; people are remembered. But how many of the numberless dead are honoured this way? These tombstones are the exception, not the rule. The real message of the beautiful Protestant Cemetery seems to be: Some lives matter. More pass away unmarked. In his book *A Night to Remember*, Walter Lord recalls that on April 14, 1912 *The New York American* sadly informed readers that tycoon John Jacob Astor was dead. He perished, the paper reported, in the sinking of the Titanic. Deep in the story it was also noted that as many as 1,800 others may have been lost. 1,800 Bar-Kays.

My mother has no grave or memorial stone. Nor would she have wanted one. Such grandiosity would have made her spin in that grave like a jet turbine. In the twenty-first century, a large resting place is hard to justify anyway. Our supply of land is finite—some cemeteries are already recycling plots. Do you really want to replace your carbon footprint with a dirt one?

Besides, a body buried in a closed casket does not really return to the soil as the poets suggest. There's not enough oxygen, and the human body is too large and too watery to be consumed by the right sort of micro-organisms. The body rots, but rich, black loam does not result—just a foul mess. So a Swedish company called Promessa Organic has developed a method of human composting. After death you will be freeze-dried to remove body moisture, then broken up like a tray of ice cubes and buried, close to the surface, in a biodegradable, aerated box. You'll be nourishing local plant life within the year.

As for cremation, it's not exactly environmentally friendly either. There's the cremation process itself, which requires tremendous heat. On average, a human cremation sends 550 pounds of carbon dioxide into the heavens. Even scarier is the vaporization of mercury fillings. According to a 2005 study cited on the U.S. Environmental Protection Agency website, cremation released 6,600 pounds of mercury into the atmosphere that year alone.

Good old Mom was clearly planning ahead for a greener demise. Losing all her teeth at an early age removed the need for fillings, mercury or otherwise. And considering her weight, reducing Mom to ashes might have been accomplished with a bag of charcoal briquets from Canadian Tire. Mom did not want to be trouble.

Yet if we ever completely eliminate the traditional graveside ritual, something archetypal will be lost. Hollywood would never stand for it. In a future without cemeteries and burial how will they stage that crucial scene in which sombre mourners gather, with one hiding a guilty secret behind dark glasses? You don't get that with cremation.

There is an appealing quality to a gravestone, and more particularly to an epitaph. Like the dream of a huge wedding celebration, it's an ideal that represents a moment of passage and transition, a statement about life's enduring meaning. It's hard to let go of that final spotlight opportunity, that grand question savoured in moments of morbid narcissism: what do I want on my tombstone?

What would we have put on Mom's? How would we have proclaimed our love?

It's traditional for a gravestone to be inscribed with verse. When I think of what our mother accomplished a famous poem does come to mind. It is "This Be The Verse," by English poet Philip Larkin, which starts like this:

They fuck you up, your mum and dad.
They may not mean to, but they do.

He does cut the poor folks some slack a little later, adding: *But they were fucked up in their turn.*

That depressing cycle does not hold true for everyone. Still, it is recognizable to millions. And my mother's experience might very well have fit right in. Victimized by her own mother, she was by Larkin's lights poised to pass it on, to become a meddling, manipulative guilt machine. She didn't. She broke the chain.

Philip Larkin can count himself lucky. He did not become a famous poet for his upbeat attitude. Larkin is reported to have said that for him, deprivation served the same poetic purpose that daffodils did for William Wordsworth. Given a happier view of parenting and life in general, what path would Larkin have taken? Greeting-card verse? A career that saw him named Britain's great-est postwar writer in a 2008 *Times* survey would have been stillborn had Larkin been born a Burgess.

As a description of family life Larkin's "This Be The Verse" has become a modern classic. As an epitaph for Joan Burgess, though, it would be problematic. We'd have to add a postscript to make clear that our mother was the exception, a woman who defied Larkin's pattern. Some-thing along the lines of, "I know you are, but what am I?"

Too complicated for a headstone, really. Better to inscribe a simple statement of tribute. But what?

"Here lies Joan Burgess, our beloved mother; bet she was better than yours."

Too competitive.

"Here lies Joan Burgess; if you ever met her mother, you'd be leaving flowers here right now."

I like it. She wouldn't.

"Here lies Joan Burgess—one tough mother."

No.

"Here lies Joan Burgess; her ordinary life became a medium for the extraordinary."

The simple truth, whether or not she realized it.

As it is we have only that park bench, inscribed: "Mom and Dad—it's been 50 years. So sit." That one she got to see. And modest though she was, she loved it.

EVERY DAY I spend in Rome begins the same way. I leave the Hotel Orlanda near Termini Station and head toward Piazza della Repubblica for my morning coffee. On the way I pass along a quiet little street that empties into the square. Barely longer than its name, Via delle Terme di Diocleziano is shaded by orange trees. That shade is a precious thing in a hot Roman summer, and makes the little street a logical place for the used-book, magazine, and movie stalls that line its north side. You can find items here not seen in the shops that crowd the Pantheon or Trevi Fountain—everything from Italian-language Batman comics, to pulp Westerns, to bits of Fascist history not found in more reputable spots.

I stop in front of a rack displaying a fascinating series of postcards—reproductions of Italian propaganda posters from the Second World War. A thuggish Jew in a Star of David coat standing before the New York skyline, fist outstretched; a leering black soldier laden with plunder in a church where the crucified Christ leans over in the rubble; a brutish black G.I. draping his arm around the Venus de Milo marked with a two-dollar price tag. (Note to Italian propagandists: The French already plundered that one.)

The proprietor wanders over. Marco is a balding, stocky man with an expired cheroot clenched in his teeth. "You understand, I must be careful about how I display these things," he says. "Some people misunderstand. But pictures like this tell you more about the time than an entire book. It's economy of energy."

Marco comes from warrior stock. "I am from San Giorgio del Sannio," he tells me, "where many Roman legions were defeated."

"My ancestors came from Scotland," I reply. "We were known to scrap a bit ourselves."

"Scotland!" Marco cries. He reaches onto a shelf and pulls out an old book. It is greenish-brown, wrapped in plastic and sealed with bits of old tape, illustrated with a painting of a mountain lake. The cover reads *Loch Lomond & The Trossachs; painted by E.W. Haslehust, R.B.A.; described by George Eyre-Todd.* Inside, a dedication in faded pen is dated August 1924, two years before my mother was born.

Whether by luck or through an instinctive genius, Marco has struck a major chord.

"There's a song about Loch Lomond," I tell Marco. "Do you know it?"

His cheroot curls slightly northward in an expectant grin. So for the first time since those nights in the hospital room when my lullaby was broken and unsettled by my mother's laboured breath, I sing "Loch Lomond." It's one of the only songs I really know how to sing.

By the time I finish, Marco's eyes have narrowed, taking on an aspect of shrewd appraisal worthy of Simon Cowell. "I can hear when a man sings a song a certain way," he says.

He hands me the book. "This is a gift."

Turn left at Piazza della Repubblica, and there is Via Nazionale, sloping to the southwest. In the morning sun, the winged chariots of Il Vittoriano monument are framed against the horizon. Strolling downhill on one of those fine mornings I find the street blocked off about halfway down. A little crowd stands behind barricades, looking down the empty street. "Giro d'Italia," a man in a panama hat explains.

Italy's biggest bike race is wrapping up. I've never seen a bike race in person before. I stand waiting for a surging pack of bikes and brightly clad riders to charge into view. Finally a single rider appears—one bright little rainbow swinging around the bend and up the hill, followed by a support car. Minutes later another rider and another car, and then another, each riding alone. The man in the panama hat explains again: "Time trials today."

Time trials—each rider against the clock. Your starting place is irrelevant; nor do you win by crossing a set finish line ahead of the other riders. It's you against a stopwatch, travelling the distance as best you can.

So far my Italian sojourn has been wonderful. A highlight was the week spent with a tiny rented Alfa Romeo, exploring the hill towns that lie behind the Italian Riviera, close to the French border. On a continuum of car-rental situations, with driving to a management seminar in Brownsville at one end, this would be at the other. Some towns you find on a map, but the best ones you find by mistake. Bajardo was a hidden hamlet at the end of a randomly chosen road. I wandered its stone ramparts, sat alone in a roofless chapel ruin, then idled at a small café atop the main street while the locals wandered from table to table, visiting. Soon a woman appeared escorting her elderly mother. The small, white-haired lady moved from group to group, greeting her friends while clinging to her daughter's arm. I buried my face deep into my day-old copy of the *International Herald Tribune*. It was embarrassing to sit there among strangers, crying.

And yet such moments have been fairly rare. Disturbingly rare, it seems to me. My emotions are a mystery. There's no manual for personal grief, and I'm not sure what I expected. Nonetheless there is something unsettling about my reaction to Mom's death. I seem to be taking it too well.

Lynn was there at the moment of death and described her feelings to me later. "I felt nauseous," she said. "Seeing Mom going and I couldn't do anything—it made me ill."

I wonder at that. I sobbed when I saw Mom's body. But there was little in my subsequent reaction that could be described as anguish. Compared with Lynn and Les, my response has been matter-of-fact.

There's an expectation that our grief will function as tribute. Our pain will be in proportion to our love. No one mattered to me more than my mother. Now that she is gone I think about her every day. The trigger might be a little white-haired lady in Bajardo, but usually just a mundane recollection; other times simply a reflexive reminder that she is gone. Yet I am not shattered by her death. My life has continued, and now here I am in Italy, scandalously enjoying myself. It makes me uncomfortable. It doesn't seem right.

MY FRIEND COLEEN, a TV news anchor from Vancouver, meets up with me in Rome. I am joining her for dinner at a little spot called L'Orso 80. The antipasti platters offer more than you can eat for a very reasonable price. It's a little like being adopted by someone's Italian grandmother for an evening.

Coleen has warned me that this will be no ordinary dinner.

John Caspar is a co-worker of Coleen's, and his wife, Sienna, a good friend. The couple has been on an Italian tour along with their two sons, Grant and Rylan. They have been in Paris and Tuscany, and visited Sienna's almost-namesake Italian town of Siena. Rome is the last stop on their family vacation. Soon they will be returning to Vancouver, where they will wait for John to die.

The trip was originally scheduled as a romantic, kid-free jaunt through Europe to coincide with a Paris conference that Sienna, a geriatric nurse, was scheduled to attend. The plan changed the day John was diagnosed. It was stage-four cancer—tongue base, commonly called "smoker's and drinker's cancer." John neither smoked nor drank, but there's no appeals court. His case was terminal. "We sat the boys down," Sienna says, "and told them that they each got to pick a lifetime memory with John. Both boys are in French immersion in school and Grant had earlier lamented the fact that neither John nor I spoke any French yet we weren't going to bring the boys with us. So Grant's wish was to turn our Paris trip into a family affair. My wish for a lifetime memory with John was to go to Siena, Italy, a place I had wanted to see. We decided to add Rome, Pisa, and San Gimignano."

So far everything has gone miraculously well. The family is taking full advantage of what grace the situation affords. Before the trip there was a huge party in Vancouver, with old friends and relatives flying in from all over to celebrate John's life and say their goodbyes. The family's European trip was planned as a final indulgence. It has been everything they hoped.

John sits across from me at the long table. He is forty-nine, with glasses, greying hair, and an arguable resemblance to actor Denholm Elliott. He is cheerful and animated. The only evidence of his illness is his skin—blotchy and peeling—but that might just as easily be the aftermath of a long day under the Tuscan sun. One other clue: John isn't eating. Instead he takes occasional sips of water from a little bag that looks like a wineskin. Intensive radiation therapy to his neck and throat has damaged his salivary glands. His taste buds too—there would be no point in his sampling the array of homey Italian dishes covering the length of the table. That joy has gone on ahead of him. For John the pleasure of dinner is now the pleasure of company.

Dinner is lively and fun, if understandably touched by a sense of the surreal. Here is a social situation to flummox the sagest advice columnist. How do you engage with a man you are meeting for the first time over dinner, knowing that any further or deeper connection will be rendered impossible by his imminent death?

The answer is provided by the family's gracious example. It is only necessary to follow their lead. They are frank and open, talking as easily about their situation as they do about their lovely rented villa in the Tuscan countryside.

At the big farewell party in Vancouver, John encountered an old acquaintance. "This was a guy I had wanted to reconnect with for years," John says. "But he had always put me off when I suggested we get together. Now here he was at the party, looking a little sheepish. He asked, 'Any chance of having that coffee now?' I told him, 'Tom, if I have a chance to meet up with you in November, I'd love to do that.'" As Tom and all of the other guests knew, doctors had told John he was unlikely to live past October.

"Tom nodded," John recalls. "He understood what I was saying. I wasn't trying to be nasty. It's just that I had to prioritize. I had to make time for the people who were there for me."

Too soon we stand outside the restaurant on the cobblestones of Via Orsini. I have pretty much grasped that any social awkwardness on my part is not particularly important in this context. All the same, it is a genuine struggle to think of an appropriate farewell. "John," I finally say, "I hope you get to keep that November coffee date."

We shake hands and part.

John goes into a rapid decline not long after the family's return home. This time the doctors had it right. He dies on October 9, 2009.

It will be five months before I meet Sienna again. On a drizzly December evening she joins Coleen and I for dinner in a Vancouver Chinatown restaurant. Sienna is a strong woman, with a successful career and two young sons to raise. Keeping it together after her husband's death has been important to her. But as she carries on, dealing with her private grief, Sienna has found herself running up against popular notions of a widow's suitable response. "People expect you to go to pieces in an obvious way," she says. "If you don't visibly lose control of yourself they think you're cold."

Here, I realize, is the person to talk to about my own situation. I want to understand: Why am I not devastated?

A couple of years ago I was a regular at a restaurant on Vancouver's Robson Street, the kind of casual food-and-drink place known in Japan as an *izakaya*. For years I had been smitten with K, one of the managers there. One day I decided to ask her out, against the advice of friends who warned me that, no matter how lengthy the acquaintance, the warmth of a professional waitress is only a required pose.

I asked her to dinner. That look of ardent desire I had craved appeared in her eyes. It was directed at the floor, which she was clearly imploring to open up and swallow her whole. I have never seen a human being squirm with such exquisite discomfort.

I went home to my apartment. Leaving the lights off I lay down on the floor. I felt about as devastated as possible in my poor capacity to feel. Mortified, humiliated, crushed.

Now I ask my dinner companions: "Why would I experience utter devastation at being rejected by a waitress—and greet the death of my own mother with relative calm and acceptance?"

"It's ego death," Sienna replies. "Your ego was crushed when you asked that woman out. With your mother, your ego was not at stake. It sounds like there were no lingering issues between you—no conflicts unresolved, or things unsaid. So the death of your mother didn't give you that same sort of pain."

My mother had a husband and five children. Each of us experienced her differently. Each of us forged a relationship that was unique in each of our lives, and different in turn from the others. My mother and I had a relationship that belonged only to us, with its own rules and dynamics. So would my grief differ from the pain of my siblings, and that of my father.

We may have started out in a pack. But ultimately each of us would travel alone, looking back once in a while to confirm the reassuring presence of that support vehicle, out of the way but always keeping pace. Gone now. But tomorrow, time trials continue.

20

GOODBYE,
CHRISTMAS TOWN

ONE THOUSAND three hundred and five
miles from Vancouver to Brandon. A
long drive, especially when your car is old enough to vote.
BMW calls it the Ultimate Driving Machine, but after
twenty years it's just another elderly Bavarian.

Most will tell you all the good parts of the journey are
in the first half—the Okanagan Valley, the Cascade Range,
and the magnificent Rockies. But the highlight of my
drive usually comes late on day one, when night has fallen
along the length of the Trans-Canada and I finally burst
free of the claustrophobic mountains into foothill country. I pull the reliable old *frau* onto the shoulder, step out
and stare upward. My hometown is still a couple of provinces away, but already I experience a powerful sense of
return, of home. Spread above me, across the clear prairie
night, are the stars. All of them. No mountains to impose
themselves, no city lights to whitewash the deep blue
firmament. The Milky Way is frozen vapour, stretching

almost to the southern horizon. We get a mere sampling in the big city.

Next day's drive on that prairie highway is a long chase after a shimmering, evaporating pool. Most of the stately old grain elevators are gone, but the freight trains still roll between fields of yellow canola and golden wheat and sometimes even a dry lake of blue flax. A little bit of country music, a lot of Loverboy, and then hours at a time when the AM radio plays nothing but the thunderstorms that crackle on the horizon.

I cross Alberta and Saskatchewan into Manitoba. There, just past the town of Virden, I meet an eager young recruit of the RCMP who's determined to prove that Manitoba has the highest speeding fines in the country, regardless of whether a man might be hurrying home to visit his anxious and bereaved old Dad.

The final miles take me along Highway 1A, the old road that once led voyagers to the welcoming arms of the Starlight, now Casablanca, Motor Hotel. These days the first significant structure on the western edge of town is my new destination—Riverheights Terrace. Crossing that final flat stretch of farmland I am suddenly aware of the scene as it appears from Dad's third-floor balcony—the empty fields, the ribbon of road, and the BMW, not quite at the point where the whining tires will cross the sonic horizon. This is my first visit since Mom's death.

Now I am standing at the door of Dad's apartment. What I see leaves me stupefied.

Riverheights Terrace has grown on me. Like most relative youngsters my attention was initially focused on the bingo and the gossip. But even before Mom died my feelings had changed. Residents of this little three-storey community understand illness, difficulty, and grief. They know the drill. They help out. There's a woman named

Lorna on staff, an indefatigable wonder whose paid work involves cleaning and serving—her mother-hen fussing over the Riverheights brood comes at no extra charge. Some of the residents turned out for the funeral, and the expressions of sympathy and support were sincere. I am glad Dad lives here.

It's true that they boil a piece of broccoli until it loses structural integrity. And some of the framed prints along the hallways are a half-step up from dogs playing poker. But no one's forcing you to play bingo or carpet bowl if you don't want to. Residents feel it's a pretty good place to be.

Still, pain stalks these hallways. There's no exterminator they can call about that. As I stand before Dad's new one-bedroom apartment I am looking at that pain, spelled out.

Riverheights apartment doors come equipped with nameplates to identify the occupants. Our old nameplate read "Bill and Joan Burgess." Someone has taken a saw and sliced out the middle. Now Dad's door is marked by two broken fragments. "Bill Burgess," it says, but with an abrupt break in the centre.

As it turns out it wasn't the work of some grim hall monitor. Dad did it himself. Always the determined, if somewhat graceless, handyman. "I thought I'd better change it," he says sheepishly.

A lot of things have changed for Dad. His eyesight is just one of them. Watching hockey with him was bad enough when he couldn't remember what colour of uniform to cheer for. Now, thanks to macular degeneration, he can barely see the uniforms. "Can you really follow this? How do you see the puck? They need a bigger puck."

"Dad," I reply, "you say the same thing during NBA games. They could play hockey with a basketball and it wouldn't matter."

TV sports and sunsets are the main events on Dad's schedule these days. He has developed an evening tradition. "When it's close to sunset, I pour myself a Scotch and sit rocking by the window," he tells me. "Mom's trophy is framed against the sky. If I rock back and forth a little it even looks like her leg is kicking."

Plans have been made. Once my mother's ashes are joined by her husband's they will be spread together on a wooded lakefront path not far from our beloved old cottage in Clear Lake. But it is another, fuller reunion that preoccupies Dad these days. In conversations he often circles around to the same question. "If we are pure spirit," he asks, "how will I recognize her on the other side?"

Dad is a theologian whose habitual spiritual musings have suddenly been transformed into the most immediate of concerns. He has spent years reading the works of Marcus Borg and Bishop John Shelby Spong. Now he parses their words with the urgency of a contract lawyer. One day he calls, sounding down. He's been fretting about a recent Spong interview published in the *United Church Observer*. "Spong is saying there's no point in kidding people about heaven," Dad says. "He says it's a false comfort. I know what he is saying. But it's hard to hear that now."

Dad and I have taken a lot of pleasure in our theological debates over the years. I have always taken the skeptic's view. Earthly institutions must not be held hostage to the dictates of ancient scriptures and superstitious beliefs, I proclaim with index finger wagging aloft. For conservative clerics the afterlife is both carrot and stick, the threat and reward that impels compliance.

But the debates have lost their sport now. This is no longer an argument I want to win. Dad has enough doubts anyway. "You can see," he tells me ruefully, "how people construct their beliefs out of necessity."

Yet the great thing about the afterlife is, it's an unresolvable argument. You can't Google the facts.

I can at least Google Spong. I find the *Observer* interview online. It turns out to be a winning case for the defense. "Look, Dad—Spong just says he doesn't want to tell bereaved people that their loved one is 'sitting on a cloud somewhere.' But later, the interviewer asks: 'The average person in the pews wants to know this: 'When I die, is there anything more? Will I know my family, my friends, my loved ones?' How do you answer that?' And Spong replies: 'This entire book [*Eternal Life: A New Vision*] is an attempt to say yes. The person I am is so deeply shaped by powerful, life-giving relationships. If I share in God's eternity, they have to be part of that. I can't get beyond that.'

"So there you go, Dad. Spong believes you'll see Mom again. Just no clouds."

Dad seems pleased to have the good bishop back in his corner. To his credit, he is not grasping at any old straw. When Jock buys him an audio book of *90 Minutes in Heaven*, the bestseller in which Don Piper describes his near-death experience as the fulfillment of his Christian faith, Dad is not impressed. "Sounds like a Baptist Sunday sermon," he grumbles.

His children would like to deny him the reunion he craves. By summer 2009, however, it is looking imminent. Dad is back in hospital.

The diagnosis this time: aortic dissection, a type of aneurysm that involves leakage between the walls of the aorta. It can lead to almost instantaneous death— 50 percent of cases never even reach the hospital. It's yet another terrifying addition to our growing medical lexicon. Many parents cherish the fond hope that their children will someday acquire a medical education. But not this way. We're like jailhouse lawyers, self-taught in the prison library.

Lynn gets to Brandon first. "The ER doc tells me Dad is resting okay," she says over the phone. "Then he says to me, 'He's quite a delightful guy.'"

She gives an exasperated snort. "Like we don't know?"

By the time I get to the hospital Dad looks pretty good, for a man with the sword of Damocles dangling over his head. He's anxious to get out. But there are still concerns. His medical file mentions a problem with dementia.

Dad strikes me as impatient, but not particularly demented. I ask a nurse what it's about. "It's in his file," she says, "He has been diagnosed with Alzheimer's."

But what has he been doing lately? "Well," she says, "when staff have been trying to get him out of bed to take some exercise, he keeps asking for his walker."

His walker—yes. It helps him walk. "That doesn't seem irrational," I say.

"We want to be careful," the nurse tells me. "He's been diagnosed with dementia." A perfect circle: The Alzheimer's diagnosis suggests that his actions will be suspect; and his actions are found to be suspect because of the diagnosis. Like they always told us in school, once you get a reputation it's hard to shake.

Happily, the consensus is now that Dad is in so much trouble it doesn't much matter where he is. So we're going home. There's an exit interview with Doc Molecule. "Live your life," he tells Dad. "You could go anytime. If you have a rupture we'd have to take you into Winnipeg and we'd never get you there in time. So just enjoy yourself."

Not bad advice. All the same, hearing a message of doom from Doc Molecule seems oddly comforting.

"Either way, it's okay," Dad tells me. "If things go wrong I will see her again."

There's not much point arguing with Molecule about the Alzheimer's issue, but I do anyway. It's how we roll. His confident diagnosis is in itself evidence of hubris—diagnosis of Alzheimer's always involves guesswork, and autopsies regularly prove that supposed cases were mis-identified. Vascular dementia, caused by just the sort of heart problems Dad has experienced, is responsible for many of the same short-term memory problems often ascribed to Alzheimer's. A 2010 British study showed GPs commonly mistake one condition for the other. Stud-ies of a new spinal fluid analysis procedure hold promise, but as of now diagnosing Alzheimer's is still a crapshoot. And crap is just what we expect from this quarter.

Yet a growing body of anecdotal Dad-related evidence suggests that it may be necessary to take a very painful step. I may be forced to agree with his doctor.

Dad's memory holds information like a monkey holds playing cards. "I enjoy reading about the baseball games in the paper next day," he tells me one night while we're watching baseball, "because I've forgotten what happened."

We're all engaged in a game of trying to gauge Dad's true abilities. It's difficult. His familiar short-term for-getfulness occasionally shades into something more troubling. One day while we're looking through scrap-books together he asks me, "When was Steve born?"

The vultures are circling. A vigilant bank employee cancels Dad's credit card after telephone solicitors ped-dling miracle Chinese tea succeed in getting his security code from him.

These visits are gradually evolving from the old rou-tine of eating and chatting and enjoying each other's company, to something more like babysitting. On a visit to Clear Lake one day Dad and I stop in at Poor Michael's Bookshop and Café, owned by our friends Murray and Lei.

Dad heads for the men's room while I stick my nose in the paper. A few minutes later I look up to see Murray leading Dad back through the front door. He'd gotten lost on the way back from the bathroom and gone looking for me outside.

With Dad there's no telling what random bytes of the data stream will stick and which will slide on past. It's an odd dynamic—the conversations we have are roughly the same, the interactions apparently normal. Two minutes later it may well be gone. Repeat the information and it seems for all the world he is hearing it for the first time. And yet you cannot simply assume that Dad's brain is a bottomless bucket. He remembers a significant amount—there's just no telling what. So you simply keep talking, having ordinary conversations, all the while remembering to take nothing for granted. It involves overcoming reflexes built up over a lifetime, unlearning the assumption that a question answered will stay answered for more than sixty seconds, or that simple instructions will produce meaningful results ten minutes later.

Chronically forgetting the stories he told yesterday, Dad tells them again as if they had just occurred to him. And since the stories are almost always the same, his obsessions are clear. "Did I tell you about the times Mom came to rescue me?" he asks. "Once when I was in Winnipeg, taking a medical study program..."

"Once when we were in Belgium on our European trip, we were going down to dinner and Joan was wearing her favourite dress—a long blue and white one. It looked so beautiful. We were walking along the wide hallway that led down to the dining room and there was an older lady coming along. She stopped us—she was a complete stranger—and she said to Mom, 'I just have to tell you how beautiful you look.' A complete stranger."

Dad will tell me that story almost every day if I don't stop him. I stop him about half the time.

Failing eyes and failing memory are a truly cruel combination. Dad doesn't deserve to star in the horrible little comedies that now play regularly at his apartment. Bad memory? He must write things down in order to remember them. Bad eyes? He can't read what he just wrote. It leads to moments like this: Dad is scanning his day-timer. It is August 19. A July 24 appointment was written down in felt pen. The black marker leaked through the page, making meaningless black splotches on the calendar square for August 7. "What's this here?" Dad asks.

"It's nothing Dad. Just felt pen that bled through the paper."

"Are you sure? What's the date? Is it still July?"

"No Dad, it's August now. Today's August 19."

"August! It can't be August! What's this written down here?"

"Just ink, Dad—just blotches."

"Are you sure? What does it say?"

Etc.

Had I recorded my last attempt to read an address to him over the phone, the transcript could make you weep. Leaving phone messages or sending emails has become pointless—he can't see the keyboards, remember the passwords, work the devices. A fancy new computer sits on his desk like a dead stump in a wheat field. Once he complained to the Riverheights manager that his TV wasn't working. The manager came up to have a look and discovered that Dad was trying to change channels with the cordless telephone.

Discipline is another major issue, but the problem here is not really medical. Dad used to possess an iron will. It was his wife. Now he'll eat ice cream three times a day if it's offered, and as a result resembles a shoplifter attempting to steal a watermelon. He gives himself permission for a few too many Scotches when twilight comes. If it hasn't come by 3 p.m., he might take an advance. There is some family concern being expressed about his liquor intake. But on the bright side, when he drinks, he stops eating.

Memory gone, eyes fogged, and yet he is still essentially himself. As Donna Hamm puts it, "He presents well."

Even if it's true that the brain is being hollowed out, the facade seems unchanged. Upbeat, gregarious, loving, loveable. Dad's final days, months, or years will not resemble Mom's in that way, at least. We lost her by degrees. With Dad the loss will be sudden and unbearably sharp.

Morbid thoughts are unavoidable now. What to say about him, when the time comes to speak?

The tradition of eulogy suddenly seems unfair. Anybody who can afford a funeral gets one. Nice things are said of the deserving and undeserving alike.

I appreciate the obituaries run by British papers when a prominent figure dies—not cruel, but not flinching from the facts either. Some obituaries are easily written. Tsutomu Yamaguchi, who died in January 2010, was the only person officially recognized as having survived the atomic blasts at both Hiroshima and Nagasaki. In the face of that awe-inspiring combination of bad and good fortune, the death notice writes itself.

Other obits are trickier. Michael Jackson: Pop wunderkind, vessel for breathtaking gifts physical and creative; mask-wearing, baby-dangling eccentric, accused child molester. There's the challenge of the eulogist at its starkest. And we are each of us Michael Jackson, if not to the same extreme.

For the unremarked and generally unremarkable, the job of the eulogist is difficult, and thus out come the clichés. He lived, did his best, left grieving family and friends. True or not, it will be said.

What can I add about my father? How to underline his goodness? Will it be necessary to resort to slander, insulting other recent dead for the sake of contrast? Bad form, I suppose. But Bill Burgess is deserving. My father is simple, in the best sense of the word—honest, open, straightforward, uncomplicated, good. He's earned his tributes.

I once believed I was almost nothing like my father. It seemed to me I was my mother's son. I understood her emotional reactions, felt we were made of the same stuff. If there is one educational thread to my adult life, it has been the process of discovering how much I am also like my Dad, and how lucky that makes me. Some vestige of his buoyant optimism has lifted me; my interface with the world resembles his. His essential decency may be available to me more by example than by heredity. Regardless I am proud and grateful to be my father's son. When the time comes that's what I can say.

For now Dad's aorta is a valiant little vessel. He is resolutely refusing to drop dead. And so we have a decision to make.

Christmas is coming. The prospect of a Yuletide holiday at Riverheights—just the two of us, a tree, and a painful void—does not seem quite the thing. Instead we'll go east. Lynn and family are in Toronto, Jock and another happy quorum of grandchildren close by in Mississauga. It only makes sense. We'll fly in separately, and Lynn will find places for us somewhere.

So it's goodbye, Christmas Town. Not the last change coming, nor the worst. Just another unfamiliar station on the road. When you're a kid you pray for Christmas to hurry up and arrive. But the damn things keep coming, like the marching broomsticks of the sorcerer's apprentice. Finally the only thing you want from Santa Claus is a break.

That's the truth behind Dickens's Christmas tale. The terrifying Spirit of Christmas Yet to Come leads Scrooge to his final resting place, and the old man falls to his knees in fear. Scrooge begs for the chance to change the future, and his wish is granted. But the Spirit's reminder still stands. Ultimately, all our futures converge. Like Scrooge we can only seize the day, and the next, and the next, as long as they're still on offer. That sentiment may never end up on a festive card, coming from a wisecracking reindeer. But if you need a reason to have yourself a merry little Christmas, it's the best one I can think of.

Beyond that, who knows? I can't convince myself of a heaven. I don't want to wrap myself in comforting myths. We are all best served by looking at matters clearly, constantly vigilant of the encroachment of wishful thinking.

But for the purposes of discussion I am only too happy to leave the question open. It's only necessary for me to acknowledge my humble place in the universe and to admit there are things I cannot know. And that clears the way for harmless, even joyful speculation.

There have been so many attempts over the years to illustrate a heaven, to imagine some scenario more satisfying than an enervating sea of white clouds and white wings and free jukeboxes offering nothing but harp solos. One of my favourite versions came from a 1998 Japanese movie, *After Life*. In that particular vision of eternity heaven is reduced to a moment. The deceased begin their afterlives with a short stay at a sort of post-mortem way-station where the staff helps each newly dead soul select a favourite memory—a single moment of pure happiness. Then that experience is re-created in a studio, complete with the appropriate props and effects. As each subject relives his or her chosen memory, he or she disappears into it, forever to exist inside that moment, looping over and over again, always fresh in a perfect, eternal now.

I don't know what moment Dad would choose. Maybe I'm too squeamish to ask. But I know that something like this is happening to him already. As his short-term memory fails him, those old, favourite loops replay in his mind, fondly repeated in every phone call. So perhaps I can guess my father's moment of heaven.

It is in Belgium. It has been a lovely trip. He and Joan are leaving their hotel room and heading down the wide, luxurious corridor to dinner. She has put on her best dress—a long blue and white one. As they approach the majestic staircase an older lady is passing—a complete stranger. But she stops. "I just have to tell you," she says to Joan, "you look so lovely."

Joan blushes. Bill looks at his wife with joy and delight. After all, hasn't he been telling her that for years? His admiration is almost triumphant. The whole world can see it—and more than that, they understand. Elegant and graceful, with a self-possession that seems the outward expression of a wise and elevated soul, here is Joan Burgess. This is the woman he loves.

And then they are coming down the wide hall, heading downstairs. An older lady is approaching—a stranger.

ACKNOWLEDGEMENTS

I COULD NOT have written this book without coffee. My thanks to the staff and management at various locations of Caffè Artigiano around Vancouver; and to the 49th Parallel Coffee Roasters café in Kitsilano. Truly your work has helped fuel this enterprise.

The dedication of this book underlines my deep gratitude to *Swerve* editor Shelley Youngblut. In 2006 *Swerve* published my essay "I'm Santa Now." A reader requested an update; "Casablanca Christmas" appeared the following year. In 2009 Shelley published "Dance Me to the End of Love," about my mother's final days. The response from *Swerve* readers convinced Shelley, who convinced me, that I should write this book. I am very grateful to all those *Swervers*—you showed me that this could be more than just a personal family story. And most of all I thank Shelley for being one of those special magazine editors whose top priority is writers and writing.

Matthew Mallon helped shape this project early on, and I have drawn on his stories and pilfered from his vast cultural knowledge.

David Beers, another great editor, has been a mentor and guide through years of fruitless fumbling. His reward is in heaven, probably. Certainly not here.

Thanks to Mya Brown for her one-woman focus groups.

When I joined the Caspar family for dinner in Rome, Sienna did not realize she and her husband would play a pivotal role in this book. My heartfelt thanks to them both, and to my friend Coleen Christie for all her tremendous help, input, and support.

Laura Murdoch also let me tell some tales. Thanks, Laura.

It may be cheesy to thank your agent, but Rick Broadhead actually taught me how to construct a book proposal, lessons that were not directly paid for. I owe him for that.

Is it also cheesy to thank your publisher? I realize Rob Sanders is in this to make a buck. Never mind. Rob took a chance after a lot of other people said, "I really like this but the answer is no because maybe it won't sell."

Thanks to my editor, Peter Norman, whose affability robbed me of the opportunity to throw artistic tantrums. Thanks also to Lara Kordic for a fine, and fine-tooth, copyedit.

Thanks to George Clooney and President Obama. Mentioning their names here adds cachet. I'm grateful for that.

Many writers thank their spouses and say, "I couldn't have done it without you." I am proof that it is possible.

I do have siblings, though. Joe, Lynn, Jock, and Leslie helped me immeasurably. Not to start any family fights here, but when it came to quotes, anecdotes, and factual information, Lynn was the undisputed champ. I beg you all, do not let this statement interfere with the harmony of future family dinners.

My cousin John Slorance helped a lot—thanks, John. Cousin Kendall Matz was great too.

My aunt, Margaret Osborn, was very generous with her reminiscences of Slorance family life. She passed away on June 2, 2010, at her cottage overlooking Otty Lake. She was the last of the Slorance children. I was grateful for her gracious assistance and only wish there had been time to ask for more.

Outside of my own recollections, my father was the primary source of information for this book. I have tried to repay him by teaching him the lyrics to "Glow Worm," whereas our recent attempt to remember all the words to "Pennies from Heaven" was more of a research collaboration. Thanks for everything, Dad. I really hope you like it.

STEVE BURGESS is an award-winning writer and broadcaster. The former host of *@the end* on CBC Newsworld, Burgess has written for *Reader's Digest*, *Salon*, and other leading magazines. *Who Killed Mom?*, which began as an acclaimed series in *Swerve* magazine, is his first book.